Revolution:

The History of Turntable Design

Revolution:

The History of Turntable Design

Gideon Schwartz

This book is unique in that it embraces aspects of analog audio culture that are intrinsically linked to turntable design. For instance, the advent of DJ culture in the 1970s would not have flourished without the development of direct-drive turntable design—namely the Technics SL-1200. Conversely, the development of the SL-1200 stemmed directly from the feedback Technics received from DJs and the dance floor. Acoustic-era design evolved from the visions of Edouard-Léon Scott de Martinville, Charles Cros, Thomas Edison, and Emile Berliner, and the inextricable links with key musical genres and myriad analog aestheticism throughout the decades are discussed here to create a representation of the analog art form.[3]

In 1921 Thomas Edison—the inventor of not just the phonograph but also the incandescent light bulb, the Kinetograph movie camera, and electric-power distribution, accumulating 1,093 patents in the United States—was asked to name his greatest invention. His response inspired me to write this book:

Which do I consider my greatest invention? Well, my reply to that would be that I like the phonograph best. Doubtless this is because I love music. And then it has brought so much joy into millions of homes all over this country, and, indeed, all over the world. Music is so helpful to the human mind that it is naturally a source of satisfaction to me that I have helped in some way to make the very finest music available to millions who could not afford to pay the price and take the time necessary to hear the greatest artists sing and play.[4]

1857–1919: The Acoustic Era

○○ Edouard-Léon Scott de Martinville

In 1857 the Frenchman Edouard-Léon Scott de Martinville, an amateur yet inquisitive scientist, created the mechanical blueprint for every turntable built over the past 164 years. This enduring technological DNA solidified the standard of analog record playback, which is to say, a laterally moving stylus tracing a groove over a laterally cut disc. This legacy fulfilled his wish to "reproduce by a graphic trace the most delicate details of the motion of sound waves."[5] Called the phonautograph, the device was intended to reproduce a visual record of aural vibrations.[6] Its brief and inconsequential career, having been decommissioned to the National Museum of American History, Smithsonian Institution, in Washington, D.C., early after its introduction, belies the brilliance of his inventive impetus.

Scott de Martinville's experiments focused on reverse engineering the workings of the human eardrum, to "copy in part the human ear, in its physical apparatus only, adapting it for the goal I have in mind."[7] By using goldbeater's skin (the outer layer of the intestinal membrane of an ox) and boxwood to replicate the human ear's innards—namely the tympanic membrane and ossicle bones—he captured sound-wave vibrations in the mouthpiece of the device, essentially duplicating the auditory canal of a human ear. The sound waves would vibrate and then cause a stylus, in this case a stiff bristle, to etch a patterned image on lampblack paper while a hand-cranked cylinder generated the mechanical movement. On March 25, 1857, the phonautograph was awarded the French patent number 17,897/31,470.[8]

Although the phonautograph amounted to a thoroughly enchanting and compelling invention, it failed in one fundamental respect: it did not aurally play back its recordings. Instead, it created a visual representation of the inscribed recording, called a phonautogram, which Scott de Martinville argued could be read just as print or text.[9] This fundamental omission of playback capability interrupted the primary aspirations of the device, and the inventor abandoned his invention, switching his vocation to become a bookseller in Paris.[10] It would take nearly 150 years for Scott de Martinville's efforts to be unearthed and brought back to life, bestowing the phonautograph as the initial forebear of analog "written" sound reproduction.

One of Scott de Martinville's paper-recorded phonautograms, "No. 5," was the French eighteenth-century folk song "Au Claire de la Lune." It was recorded on April 9, 1860, and remained in a Parisian archive until 2008, at which time scientists at Lawrence Berkeley National Laboratory in California began working with the rag-paper recording, which measured 9 by 25 inches (22.9 × 63.5 centimeters). Using digital-imaging technology to convert the ancient code to a digital file, they succeeded in extracting sound from the soot-blackened phonautogram. Played back a century and a half after being recorded, "the voice, muffled but audible, sings, 'Au Clair de la Lune, Pierrot répondit' in a lilting eleven-note melody—a ghostly tune, drifting out of the sonic murk."[11] If Scott de Martinville had been able to listen to this phonautogram, would he have endorsed its aural playback? His goal, after all, was not sound in and of itself but "writing speech" as evidence of the musical intent.[12] This fundamental characterization would twenty years later distinguish Thomas Edison as the first person to effectively reproduce sound, preserving the historical contributions of each inventor.

0.1   ILLUSTRATIONS FROM EDOUARD-LÉON SCOTT DE MARTINVILLE'S PHONAUTOGRAPH PATENT, ISSUED MARCH 25, 1857

0.2   PHONAUTOGRAPH AFTER EDOUARD-LÉON SCOTT DE MARTINVILLE, R. KOENIG, 1865

0.3   REPLICA OF EDOUARD-LÉON SCOTT DE MARTINVILLE'S 1857 FLATBED PHONAUTOGRAPH, BUILT BY ANTON STOELWINDER, 2016

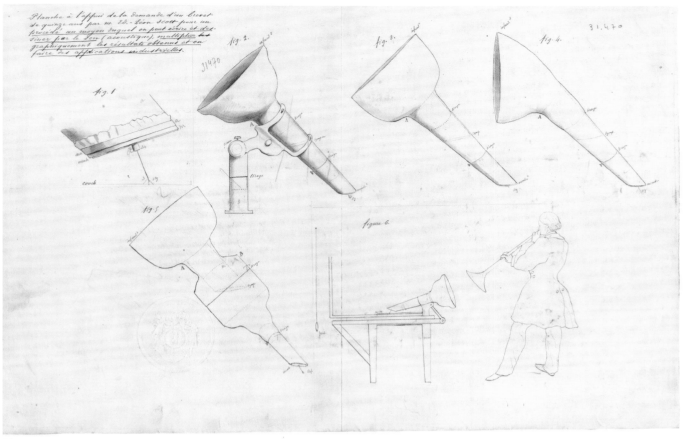

0.1

0.2

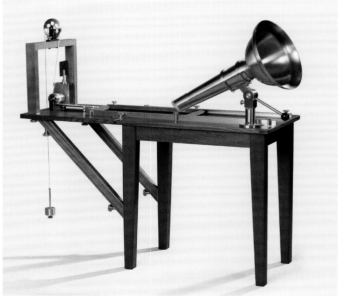

0.3

ai remi ce band On dan teur rrage cruell

no tion du déser sou teur antre brulan

de chirre quelque foi le voiiageur tremblan

il vodrai miell pour tui que teur fain dévorante

disspersa tes lamb On de sa chair palllpitannte

que de tomber vivAN dan mes terrribll main

0.4

0.5

PARLORTONE

AU CLAIR DE LA LUNE
Édouard-Léon Scott de Martinville
(PT-1001)

THE PHONOGRAPHIC ARM AND LIMITED EDITION LEG OF DUST-TO-DIGITAL

○○   Charles Cros

Twenty years after Scott de Martinville's phonautograph, another inventive Frenchman emerged who was also ensconced in the endeavor of music recording and replay. A friend of Edouard Manet, Theodore de Banville, and Paul Verlaine, the artistically and poetically inclined Charles Cros was not a likely inventor. Yet the amateur scientist can be credited with conceiving the spinning disc as a medium for sound reproduction.

On April 18, 1877, Cros wrote a paper delineating a process of recording and reproducing sound. Submitted to the French Academy of Sciences in Paris, the paper explicated a process that "consists in obtaining traces of the movements to and fro of a vibrating membrane and in using this tracing to reproduce the same vibrations, with their intrinsic relations of duration and intensity, either by means of the same membrane or some other one equally adapted to produce the sounds which results from the series of movements."[13] While this description was essentially consistent with Edison's contemporaneous thinking, Cros's application differed in two critical respects: he specified a disc as opposed to Edison's cylinder, as well as tracing sound waves on lamp-blackened glass, followed by photoengraving the tracings into reliefs or indentations, in contrast to Edison's tinfoil system (which will be discussed later).

Cros's letter was sent to the Academy on April 30, 1877, but it remained unopened until December 5, 1877. While the delay in response is mysterious, it is believed that the poet was attempting to raise funds to secure a patent, albeit unsuccessfully, a somewhat unsurprising result for an unproven quasi-scientist. Interestingly, on October 10, 1877, the scientific journal *La Semaine du Clergé* published an article by Abbé Lenoir discussing the mechanisms proposed by Cros. It was in this piece that Lenoir titled Cros's device as the "phonograph," joining two Greek roots for "sound" and "writer."[14] Emboldened by the article, Cros lobbied the Academy to reveal his sealed letter. Although the Academy eventually brought it to light in December 1877, Edison proved marginally faster in applying for a patent and executing his interpretation of the phonograph. Bestowing upon historians the tired debate of who was first to claim credit for the phonograph, it is certain that Cros was the first to envisage the machine, but Edison was the first to actually execute it. Scott de Martinville's and Cros's analog plans would find their way into later French turntable designs, such as those by Pierre Lurné and Pierre Riffaud, effectively manifesting the early inventors' unrealized potential.

0.4   EDOUARD-LÉON SCOTT DE MARTINVILLE'S INTERPRETATIONS OF PHONAUTOGRAPH INSCRIPTIONS, 1859

0.5   SINGLE-SIDED 45 RPM RECORD MADE FROM EDOUARD-LÉON SCOTT DE MARTINVILLE'S 1860 PHONAUTOGRAPH RECORDING OF "AU CLAIRE DE LA LUNE," DUST-TO-DIGITAL PARLOTONE LABEL, 2010

○○ Thomas Edison

Edison once established a premise for would-be inventors: "When you are experimenting and you come across anything you don't thoroughly understand, don't rest until you run it down; it may be the very thing you are looking for or it may be something far more important."[15] In this vein, the primary endeavor consuming Edison's inventive passion since his teen years, telegraphic repeaters, would lead him not to what he was looking for, namely a high-speed telephone transmitter, but rather to something entirely different: the phonograph.

Since the age of eighteen, Edison had been working on a machine that would record messages at one speed and retransmit them at a faster speed. The intent was to indent paper with Morse code messages and then repeat the message at any speed necessary, aiming to create an efficient and quick method of sending messages. But as Edison worked on the machine, he discovered something that would alter his inventive course: as the indented tape traveled through the device, it generated a sound that he characterized as a "light musical, rhythmic sound, resembling human talk heard indistinctly."[16] This observation would ultimately lead him away from recording telegraph messages and toward recording telephone messages. The year was 1877, and he was deeply entrenched in telephone development. Only thirty years old, he invented a carbon transmitter for Alexander Graham Bell's telephone, allowing him the financial freedom to explore his own ideas.

Encouraged by what he heard from his work on the telegraphic repeater, Edison embarked on creating a machine that could record the spoken word. That recording would then be brought to a transmitting station, where another machine would play it back and transmit the recording through a telephone line. During the development of this machine, Edison's hearing had deteriorated to the point where he could not determine loudness levels from the telephone receiver. Adapting to his disability, he fixed a needle to the diaphragm of the receiver, enabling him to see the amplitude of the signal. Simply scratching his skin with the needle would register a signal, leading Edison to deduce that the needle could scratch a paraffin-paper tape just as well to register sound.

0.6   THOMAS EDISON SPEAKING INTO A PHONOGRAPH, 1888

0.6

Entrusting his mechanic, John Kruesi, to build the initial prototype, Edison drafted a sketch outlining its parameters. The rudimentary apparatus included a tinfoil cylinder and a diaphragm with a needle affixed for recording, along with an identical diaphragm and needle for playback. Known as the hill-and-dale process, Edison's method used a needle or stylus to cut a vertical groove into the cylinder. By turning the handle on the cylinder, the needle-carved patterns of sound vibrations registered from the mouthpiece onto the metal. For playback, the process was reversed, whereby the traced groove was transmitted into the second diaphragm and emerged as sound through the mouthpiece. The hill-and-dale method would dominate early cylinder recordings, such as Edison Disc Records as well as the Pathé disc records in France, and would eventually succumb to the lateral recording technique envisioned by Cros and later championed by Emile Berliner.

But Edison's phonograph produced an inferior quality of sound, and by October 1878 it had become painfully clear that the machine provided limited utility. The sound quality was so poor that even Edison's own advertisement for the product provided a full disclaimer as to its limitations: "The adaptation of this wonderful invention to the practical uses of commerce not having, as yet, been completed in all its mechanical details, this company is now prepared to offer to the public only that design or form of apparatus which has been found best adapted to its exhibition as a novelty."[17] With his phonograph characterized as a mere curiosity, Edison—the New Jersey–based "Wizard of Menlo Park"—deserted this tinfoil apparatus in favor of the incandescent light bulb, a more enthusiastically received and financed undertaking. Not dissimilar to Scott de Martinville and Cros in France, Edison too would bestow analog creativity upon future local turntable designers. Poignantly, only fifteen miles away from Edison, New Jersey, sits VPI Industries, one of the world's current leaders in turntable design and execution.

0.7   THOMAS EDISON'S PHONOGRAPH SKETCH, NOVEMBER 29, 1877

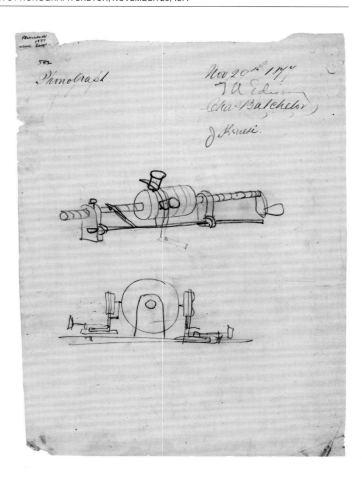

0.7

0.8

0.9

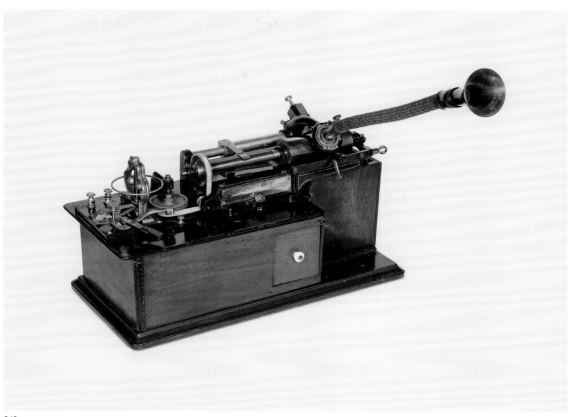

0.10

0.11

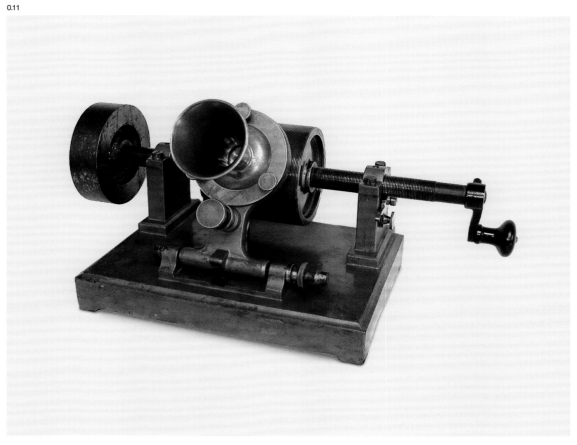

○○ Coin in Slot, and the Rise of the Columbia Phonograph Company

With Edison's withdrawal from the development of phonographic technology, other key figures decided to expand from where Edison left off. In 1886 Alexander Graham Bell, along with his cousin Chichester A. Bell and Charles Sumner Tainter, introduced the wax-cylinder-based "graphophone," forming the American Graphophone Company in 1887.[18] Although this resurrected Edison's drive to improve his invention—and generated a healthy competition between Edison and Bell—both inventors' companies were purchased by the capitalist Jesse Lippincott, who would take control of the entire talking-machine industry in the United States under the North American Phonograph Company.

Driving the newfound success of the heretofore novelty was the creation of a nickel-in-slot, pay-per-play machine, effectively an early jukebox, which served the public's desire for recorded entertainment. The early marches of John Philip Sousa along with songs from Stephen Foster helped fuel the demand.[19] Parallel to and symbiotic with this development, the recording industry arose. Created as an offshoot of the American Graphophone Company, the Columbia Phonograph Company became the primary recording and music-distribution entity, cementing its market foundation and legacy in the recorded arts. By 1893 Columbia could boast a catalog of thirty-two pages, featuring an expansive list of artists and repertoire.[20]

○○ Emile Berliner

Arriving in New York from Germany in 1870, the young and itinerant Emile Berliner worked myriad jobs. Like most new immigrants, his impetus was to survive, and he found employment in a dry-goods store in Washington, D.C., and as a bottle washer in a laboratory. What is most interesting about Berliner is how he spent his evenings: in the library of the Cooper Union in New York City. Studying physics and chemistry, he built a modest laboratory in his boardinghouse and busied himself with experiments relating to the telephone transmitter. After successfully filing a patent for a newly devised telephone transmitter, his utility to the Bell Telephone Company became apparent, as the firm paid him a considerable sum and engaged him for ongoing research. Still, Berliner's enthusiasm for the telephone was short-lived.

Coinciding and consistent with Edison's trajectory from telephone to phonograph, Berliner would similarly abandon the telephone in favor of a machine for sound recording and playback. The fundamental difference, however, was Berliner's support of a laterally moving stylus, as opposed to Edison's vertical, hill-and-dale method. Utilizing a disc instead of Edison's cylinder, Berliner would effectively unearth and materialize what Scott de Martinville and Cros envisioned earlier. Applying for his patent on September 26, 1887, Berliner distinguished his new apparatus as the "gramophone." He refined the gramophone through patented improvements into the early twentieth century.

Simultaneously with developing a machine, Berliner put equal emphasis on improving the quality and fidelity of disc records along with the stamping process, laying the duplication groundwork for the record industry to follow. He argued that his motivation was to make as many copies as desired from an original recording. And flowing from that he reasoned, "Prominent singers, speakers or performers may derive an income from royalties on the sale of their phonautograms."[21] His impassioned insight into the medium as entertainment with mass appeal served as a major catalyst for the gramophone's market resilience and eventual success over cylinder-based machines.

0.12

0.13

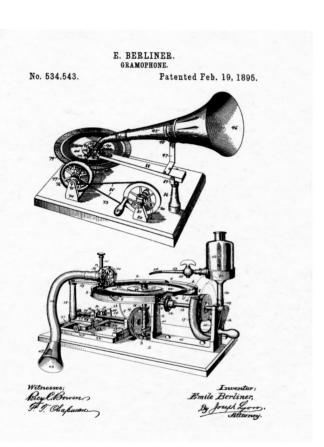

0.14

0.15

○○ The Victor Talking Machine Company

To appreciate the advent of Victor, one would need patience to untangle the legal imbroglio and complex business leveraging that preceded its creation. But in the end, Victor and its Red Seal label of music recordings would leave a lasting and enduring mark on audio recording and playback history.

As a machinist once employed by Berliner, Eldridge Johnson undoubtedly respected Berliner's patent. But by 1901 the situation was much more complex. Johnson had contributed handsomely to Berliner's invention and engineered the motor and sound box. Most compellingly, he also advanced and refined the process of disc recordings. Further, Johnson's control of the factory and sales organization balanced Berliner's exclusivity and rights to proceeds. After extensive negotiations, Berliner and Johnson decided to form a new corporation, the Victor Talking Machine Company, under Johnson's management, in which Berliner would receive 40 percent of common stock and Johnson would receive 60 percent.

By 1902, along with Johnson's many improvements to the gramophone and disc quality, one new feature would stand out: the invention of the tonearm. Johnson advanced the tonearm in order to permit the coupling of the sound box to the metal horn without having to hold its weight. It greatly reduced disc wear and considerably improved sound fidelity. Victor claimed its new device with the tonearm was "the world's greatest musical instrument."[22]

Victor's famous trademark, a terrier dog named Nipper charmingly listening to a gramophone—an image retouched by its painter Francis Barraud from his original painting that featured a cylinder phonograph—would also later serve as the logo for Victor's British Commonwealth affiliate, His Master's Voice, or HMV.[23]

On the company's recording side, the world's first classical-music label was born: Red Seal. Spearheading the idea to elevate the marketing cache of top-tier artists, Victor's agent in St. Petersburg, Russia, devised a red label that would adorn premium-priced records. This red label would eventually become synonymous with famous artists of the day, such as Enrico Caruso along with other opera singers and classical instrumentalists.[24]

0.16	VICTOR 6 PHONOGRAPH, VICTOR, EARLY 1900s
0.17	PORTABLE GRAMOPHONE, VICTOR, c.1915
0.18	PORTABLE GRAMOPHONE (WITH GEISHA REPRODUCER, C. H. GILBERT & CO.), c.1920

0.16

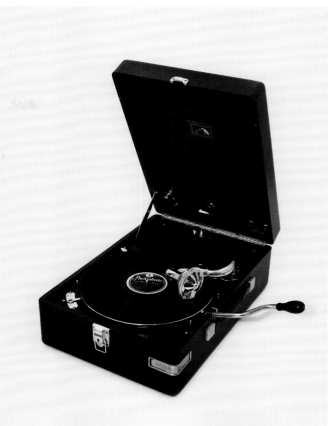

0.17

0.18

0.21

0.22

0.23

0.24

0.25

0.26

0.27

0.28

0.29

0.30

○○   Analog Culture in Europe: Pathé, Deutsche Grammophon, and Odeon

The advent of phonographs and gramophones cannot be explained solely by technical facts. Equal attention must be given to the artistic and societal factors that contributed to Europe's analog zeitgeist.

France during the Belle Époque was ready to embrace the talking machine, albeit quite unexpectedly. The lively Parisian bistro Bar Américain was an unlikely birthplace of Gallic analog roots. But the restaurant's animated and buoyant spirit would kindle the imaginations of its owners, Charles and Emile Pathé, especially after Charles witnessed an Edison phonograph at a local fair. Not unaware of the multitudes of gawkers coming to see the device, the Pathé brothers envisioned having an Edison at their bistro, drawing the crowds in a similar fashion.[25] Moving forward on the idea, they invested in a phonograph and set it up at their establishment on rue Fontaine; it did not take long for the fascinated masses to arrive. Inevitably, customers inquired about how to purchase such a machine, so the brothers built a factory in the suburb of Chatou. The Pathé Brothers Company was born, and demand for phonographs and recordings fueled its ascent. Their first phonograph was called "Le Coq," and the proud bird would soon serve as Pathé's trademark. On the recording end, Pathé could boast 1,500 cylinder titles in its 1899 catalog. But the éclat of the two brothers was evident in how a prospective buyer could actually listen to one of those many titles: in the sumptuously designed Salon du Phonographe on Boulevard des Italiens, music lovers could sample any cylinder while lounging in a plush setting. With this formula, Paris became a cultural mecca for phonographs and the recording arts. It was no wonder the Columbia Graphophone Company chose Paris as its first foreign office; the Pathé brothers can unequivocally take credit.[26]

Although Emile Berliner immigrated to the United States, he returned to Germany often, expanding his gramophone and record distribution there. In 1898 he founded Deutsche Grammophon Gesellschaft, a record label focusing on classical works.[27] Continuing to this very day, it has inarguably attained legendary status in classical circles.

0.32	"SALON DU PHONOGRAPHE," ADVERTISEMENT FOR THE PATHÉ PHONOGRAPRAPH SALON, 1899
0.33	"À LA CONQUÊTE DU MONDE (THE CONQUEST OF THE WORLD)," ADVERTISEMENT FEATURING THE PATHÉ BROTHERS, ADRIEN BARRÈRE, 1970

0.32

0.33

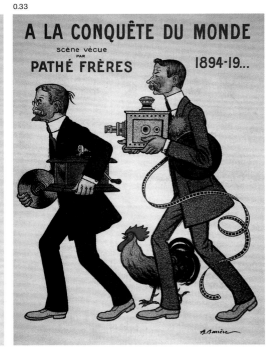

0.34

0.35

0.36

Alternatively, Germany introduced another recording label that would serve as a counterpoint to Deutsche Grammophon's exclusively classical catalog. Branching out and cultivating a global approach, Odeon could be described as the first "world music" label. With an expansive view, it exposed exotic and unknown artists to curious music lovers worldwide.[28] Founded in 1903 by Max Strauss and Heinrich Zuntz, the company borrowed the name and logo from the Odeon theater in Paris.[29] Sending agents to Asia, South America, the Middle East, and other locales, Odeon set up remote recording facilities, capturing the music of local artists. In addition to its musical appeal, Odeon's media would also become notable for both its Orientalism and Weimar Republic aestheticism. Technically, Odeon was lauded for being the first company to record a large orchestral work, along with making double-sided discs (at the time, other companies were making only single-sided discs).[30] While these were momentous achievements, Odeon's distinction rests in its ethnic musical contribution to analog culture.

0.37	"FONOTIPIA ODEON: DOUBLE FACE," ADVERTISEMENT FOR DOUBLE-SIDED DISCS, ODEON, 1904–10
0.38	EMILE BERLINER WITH HIS BROTHER JOSEPH AND WORKERS IN THE DEUTSCHE GRAMMOPHON GESELLSCHAFT FACTORY IN HANOVER, GERMANY, 1898
0.39	CATALOG DISTRIBUTED IN INDIA FEATURING ODEON RECORDS, LYRICS, AND MUSICIANS, ODEON, 1935

0.37

0.38

0.39

0.40

0.41

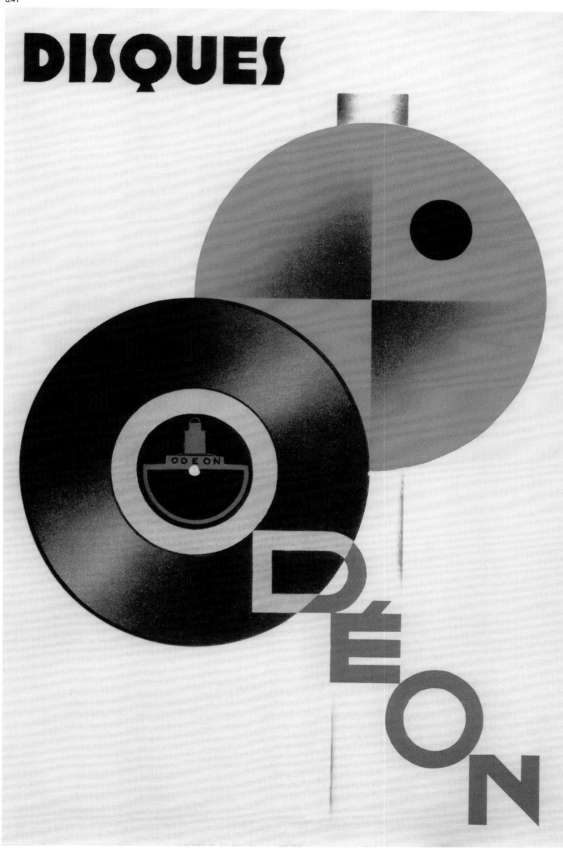

○○   Japan and the *Chikuonki*

The Japanese *chikuonki*, meaning "sound-storing machine," was not the type of device one would expect a warm welcome for in turn-of-the-century Japan. A steadfast traditional society defined the Japanese empire, but a growing fascination with the West yielded a sentiment of opening up to the outside world.

Placing a bet on that new dawning was Fred Gaisberg, an American recording engineer sent to Japan by the Gramophone Company in 1903 in order to sell the Japanese on the phonograph's glories.[31] In a hotel room in Tokyo, Gaisberg recorded the performance of musicians from the Imperial Household Orchestra and then played the recording for those in attendance. Gaisberg's success that day can be measured by the 270 Japanese titles he recorded in the span of one month after debuting his phonograph.[32] These titles were manufactured in Germany and then distributed to an eager Japanese public.

Five and seven years later, in 1908 and 1910, Japan built its first pressing plant and recording company, Nipponophone. Japan's early experience with sound reproduction would later bear fruit in its future turntable designs. In his 1933 book, *In Praise of Shadows*, Jun'ichiro Tanizaki discussed the difficulty he had with Western recording devices trying to capture the ethereal and transcendental art that is Japanese music: "Had we invented the phonograph, how much more faithfully would they reproduce the special character of our voices and our music."[33] By the 1960s Tanizaki's aspirations materialized as Japan emerged as one of the leading manufacturers of turntables, tonearms, and cartridges.

○○   The End of the Acoustic Era

By the 1920s the purest expression of analog reproduction would come to an end. The world would never again witness the mechanical preservation of a sine wave so painstakingly faithful. The inevitability of electrical progress ushered in the microphone, vacuum tubes, and, most notably, radio. Taking a back seat to the public's predilection for radio, turntables, and playback machines would take a while to fulfill the aspirations of their kaleidoscopic progenitors.

0.42–43   MODEL 35 PHONOGRAPH, NIPPONOPHONE, c.1910

0.42

0.43

1920–1949: The Early Electric Era

○○ Race Labels and Jazz, and Victor Reluctantly Recedes

By the early 1920s, a confluence of events would change the phonograph's fortunes in ways unexpected yet seemingly inevitable, as the forces of technological momentum turned the page on mechanical phonographs and acoustically recorded records.

It can be argued that a certain quiescence or dormancy had seeped into the phonograph industry. From the turn of the century and advent of the phonograph until the 1920s, few substantive changes occurred. Victor's 1921 Victrola model appeared barely changed from the original version of 1905, and the company was still banking off its "His Master's Voice" trademark along with a static Red Seal artist catalog. For years Victor had maintained the squat, hinged design of the Victrola, but the public called for a model with a flat top, similar to cabinets built by Victor's competitors, Brunswick and Sonora. Begrudgingly acquiescing to market demand for a new design, Victor eventually modified its Victrola but refused to give in entirely, in the end simply creating a variation on a theme by maintaining an elevated lid over the center of the unit. Nicknamed "the humpback," the widely mocked variation failed to sell.[34] Nonetheless, sales for Victor in 1921 topped $50,000,000, and record sales hit a healthy $140,000,000, which was four times more than record sales for 1914.[35]

Driving the continued demand was America's newfound fascination with jazz. Evolving from a culture of improvisation within smaller ensembles, jazz was a maturing musical movement that had reached commercial validation and broad cultural awareness. Early critics demonized jazz as immoral and salacious, but they could not prevent its cultural ascent and embrace.[36]

Victor was quick to sign the musicians Fred Waring and Paul Whitman while Columbia acquired Fletcher Henderson and Ted Lewis to its roster of artists. Smaller labels such as Gennett, Paramount, and Sunshine, referred to as "race labels," sought out accomplished African American musicians from New Orleans, namely Louis Armstrong, King Oliver, Kid Ory, and Jelly Roll Morton.[37] Capturing the music of Harlem's cabaret circuit and musical renaissance was Harry Pace and his Black Swan Records, the first African American–owned record label in the United States. Quickly signing Ethel Waters, known as Sweet Mama String Bean, Pace released her new song, "Down Home Blues," to immediate acclaim and sold one hundred thousand copies soon after its release.[38] Thus, jazz infused both the phonograph and record industries with renewed optimism.

This was most certainly welcomed after World War I converted Victor's Camden, New Jersey, facility into an armaments factory, which effectively halted the industrial apparatus of the acoustic era. Despite the brief postwar sales euphoria, it was clear that Victor's complacency and dogmatic adherence to its position served as a factor in undoing the growth of the phonograph. Victor also willfully ignored the imminent development of radio, failing to embrace its future promise and market viability.

0.44 RECORD LABEL FOR "SHAKE IT AND BREAK IT," HENDERSON'S DANCE ORCHESTRA, BLACK SWAN RECORDS, 1922

0.45 VICTOR TALKING MACHINE COMPANY LOGO, c.1922

0.44

0.45

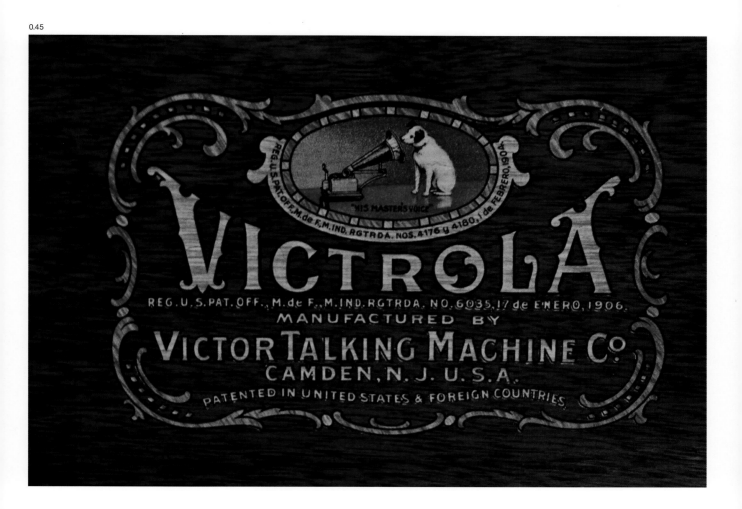

By 1922 various manufacturers were beginning to build consoles combining phonographs and radios. Both Sonora and Brunswick spearheaded this consolidated approach; Brunswick cleverly partnered with the Radio Corporation of America (RCA) to install RCA's popular Radiolas inside Brunswick's phonograph cabinets. Undeterred, Victor took a derisive position, one premised on Eldridge Johnson's reluctance in validating the radio, by designing its Victrola with an empty slot for any radio chosen by the customer. History has a way of serving up sardonic lessons, though: in this case, RCA eventually purchased Victor in 1929, naming the new company RCA Victor.[39]

0.46   "SONORA : LE MEILLEUR PHONOGRAPHE DU MONDE (SONORA: THE BEST PHONOGRAPH IN THE WORLD)," ADVERTISEMENT FOR SONORA, 1927

0.47–48   VV-300 PHONOGRAPH, VICTOR TALKING MACHINE COMPANY, 1921 (THIS MODEL, c.1922)

0.46

0.47

0.48

○○ From Acoustical to Electrical Recordings

Until the 1920s designing and creating acoustical phonographs was a precarious art. The process was imbued with a trial-and-error and learn-as-one-goes attitude. Even Victor's lead engineer, S. T. Williams, once confessed: "A complete theory connecting the great series of disjointed facts was still lacking. Development along empirical lines had reached its utmost and the art of sound reproduction had come practically to a standstill in its progress."[40]

Transitioning to a more scientific approach, both Bell Laboratories and Western Electric in the United States, along with the HMV and Columbia branches in the United Kingdom, applied physics and math in order to address the recording process. The joint developments of telephone-transmission and microphone technologies provided the tools needed to develop a framework in which sound waves could be transformed into electrical signals and then amplified to activate a recording stylus.

The key ingredient that electrical recordings, microphones, and early recording apparatuses relied upon was the vacuum tube, invented by the English physicist John Ambrose Fleming. Tapping into the earlier work of Frederick Guthrie in the field of thermionic emission, Fleming created an encapsulated glass bulb housing two electrodes, a cathode and an anode. Thermionic emission is the release of electrons from a heated element, like a cathode. As the glass bulb is a vacuum and thus has no air, a current is created from the cathode to the anode. Fleming called his invention an "oscillation valve."[41]

The American engineer Lee De Forest expanded this principle further, creating a triode, or three-element vacuum tube, called the Audion.[42] This design served broad applications. Noteworthy is the fact that it was the first device to actually amplify a signal and would thus be indispensable for all electric recording devices, until it was replaced by transistors in the 1960s.[43]

0.49	FLEMING OSCILLATION VALVES, c.1903
0.50	JOHN AMBROSE FLEMING WITH HIS OSCILLATION VALVE, 1923

0.49

0.50

○○ The Microphone

The acoustical process of recording had reached a point of increasing impracticality, and the time was ripe for a device that would revolutionize recording, radio transmission, and disc sound quality. Thomas Edison was the first to the microphone-patent finish line, but historians have credited the Englishman David Edward Hughes as the inventor of the carbon microphone. Emile Berliner, too, was influential in its development.[44] Following suit, Western Electric developed the first condenser microphone in 1916, while the British Broadcasting Corporation, with help from Alan Blumlein and Herbert Holman, perfected the Marconi-Sykes magnetophone, most famously with the HB1A and HB1E microphones.[45]

0.51   MOUNTAIN CHIEF, CHIEF OF MONTANA BLACKFEET, LISTENING TO A RECORDING WITH ETHNOLOGIST FRANCES DENSMORE, 1916

0.51

Technological advancements are one thing, but whether those advancements contributed to better-sounding early phonographs and records is another thing entirely. It took some work to convince people, who had grown accustomed to mechanical phonographs and acoustically recorded records. By 1926, however, the musical cognoscenti came on board. After listening to the newly recorded discs, Ernest Newman, the revered music critic of the London *Sunday Times*, had this to say:

> Until lately it was a little difficult to take even a good orchestral record quite seriously… They were manifestly misrepresenting the original at many points, and so could hardly give complete pleasure to musicians who knew the original; but they could still be useful to the student and lover of music whose opportunities for concert-going were limited and who could not get much pleasure or profit out of a score. All at once, however, as it seems, gramophone recording has taken an enormous step forward… Those who have heard these records for themselves will have probably felt, as I did at my first hearing of them, that at last it is possible for the musician to sit at home and get the thrill of the real thing as he knows it in the concert room. The records have their weaknesses, but they seem trifling in comparison with the great mass of their virtues. At last an orchestra really sounds like an orchestra; we get from these records what we rarely had before—the physical delight of passionate music in the concert room or opera house. We do not merely hear the melodies going this, that, or the other way in a sort of limbo of tonal abstractions; they come to us with the sensuous excitement of actuality.[46]

0.52

0.53

This quotation conveys the glowing critical affirmation of electric recordings. Analog culture of the 1920s was ready to embrace the next generation of recorded arts.

Catching up to the electrically recorded record was its counterpart, the phonograph. Initially, the mechanical phonograph was modified by Bell Labs with a newly designed exponential horn, which resulted in marked improvements in fidelity. Frequency range had been extended and performance of bass and treble ranges was dramatically improved. Despite the improvements brought by the exponential horn, electrical reproduction—utilizing an electromagnetic stylus, vacuum tubes, and speaker—eventually proved far superior to its mechanical predecessor. Western Electric engineers presented the electrical design concept to Victor, which in turn was impressed and branded it as the Orthophonic. The first demonstration of this Victrola was so momentous that it was featured on the front page of the *New York Times*, replete with accolades.[47] Quickly advancing its Orthophonic lineup, Victor would also release the world's first fully automatic record changer.

0.52	HUGHES MICROPHONE DETECTOR, DAVID EDWARD HUGHES, 1865–75
0.53	HB1E MICROPHONE, ALAN BLUMLEIN, EMI, 1931
0.54	ORTHOPHONIC VICTROLA CREDENZA, VICTOR TALKING MACHINE COMPANY, 1925

0.54

○○   The Depression and Art Deco

The electrical advancements of the mid-to-late 1920s, however, could not sustain phonograph sales into the Depression era. By the early 1930s the record business in the United States was vanquished. Considered a luxury, analog culture would take a few years and the assistance of President Franklin Delano Roosevelt's New Deal to experience a revival. In deference to the frugal times, RCA Victor released the inexpensive Duo Jr., an electric record-player attachment to radios, which aimed to incentivize record purchases and renew consumer interest.

Also sensitive to the market tenor of the Depression was Jack Kapp, who expanded the British company Decca Records to the United States with an emphasis on inexpensive records.[48] The labels Bluebird, Melotone, Perfect, Vocalion, and Okeh were also pressing cheaper records. But with an aging fan base composed of people who grew up with Edison and the phonograph, the record needed a younger demographic to stay afloat. By the mid-1930s, teenagers were moving away from Mozart and gravitating toward Benny Goodman and Duke Ellington, among other swing-era notables.[49] These new stars were sought out and signed by the savvy Edward Wallerstein of Columbia Records, serving to revitalize and diversify its catalog.

By 1941—with industry-wide discounting, jukeboxes, and a competitive marketplace—prospects for the phonograph were on an upswing. On the design side, the aesthetic of Art Deco found its way into phonograph forms, with extraordinary beauty, materials, and craftsmanship. For instance, the famed industrial designer John Vassos contributed star power and credibility to phonograph crafting of the day. In terms of the recording industry, sales had exceeded expectations that year, and there was no reason to doubt its continued ascension.

0.55	THE RECORD SHOP, PARIS, c.1930s
0.56	LA PLAQUE TOURNANTE SHOP, PARIS, THÉRÈSE BONNEY, c.1929
0.57	EXCELDA PORTABLE GRAMOPHONE, THORENS, c.1935
0.58	EXCELDA PORTABLE GRAMOPHONE, THORENS, 1931 (THIS MODEL, 1932)

0.55

0.56

0.57

0.58

0.59

0.60

0.61

0.62

0.63

0.64

0.65

0.66 "PATHÉ : L'ENREGISTREMENT ÉLECTRIQUE LE PLUS PERFECTIONNÉ (PATHÉ: THE MOST PERFECTED ELECTRIC RECORDING)," ADVERTISEMENT FOR PATHÉ, A.M CASSANDRE, 1932

0.66

0.67

0.68

0.69

0.70

0.71

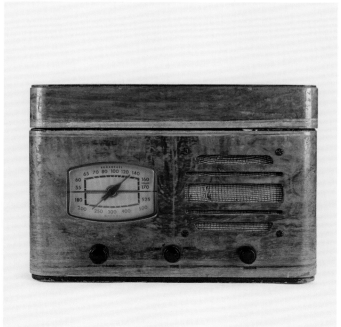

0.72

0.73

0.74

0.75

0.76

0.77

○○ World War II and Record Production

Then a war came. After the United States entered World War II, the importation of shellac, the primary ingredient in records, was cut by the War Production Board.[50] In addition, all of the nation's radio and phonograph manufacturers were forced to convert their factories to armament and war-material production. Analog culture would have to wait until June 18, 1948, when a momentous demonstration at the Waldorf Astoria hotel in New York City would convincingly resurrect the record format, ushering in a golden age of turntable ingenuity and dynamism.

0.78   "NOW FOR SOME MUSIC," ADVERTISEMENT FOR THE NATIONAL PHONOGRAPH-RECORDS RECRUITING CORPS, C. B. FALLS, 1917

0.78

1950s

○○ Turntable Design Embraces Mid-Century Ideals

The period following World War II introduced a functional and utilitarian creed that would be expressed in 1950s turntable design: elaborate consoles embellished with ornate trimmings in the Art Deco style were soon replaced by simple and uncluttered machines. Driving this change was a collective effort by industrial designers who were eager to employ mature mass-production processes to make devices with clean lines and guileless forms. Consistent with this lack of pretense, 1950s turntable design favored metal frames, yielding to a professional radio industry sentiment. Examples by such companies as A. R. Sugden, EMT, Lenco, and Garrard attest to the desire for unadorned simplicity. A notable example of this trend is the Gates Radio Company, founded in Illinois in 1922, which established itself early on as a key manufacturer of broadcast equipment. By the 1950s it introduced new broadcast-quality turntables that incorporated a novel drive system to diminish rumble, which resulted in a reduced motor speed. Prized for their high quality, Gates turntables became staples in many 1950s radio and TV stations. In concert with this movement, mid-century enthusiasm also introduced an element of fun and postwar frivolousness, with many portable record players introduced in Bakelite and colorful suitcases, famously embraced by the Collaro, Dansette, and Philips companies.

Dominating most turntable designs of the 1950s were both idler-drive and rim-drive systems. An idler drive uses a capstan shaft to drive the platter, whereas a rim drive negates a capstan in favor of a wheel that is coupled to a motor that drives the platter. With the introduction of the microgroove long-playing record that spun at 33⅓ revolutions per minute (rpm), most turntables now featured multispeed flexibility to accommodate the older 78-rpm recordings as well as the newer format with the slower speed. Adaptors and record changers were additionally introduced to accommodate new 45-rpm discs.

The new 33⅓-rpm disc, along with the 45, required a stylus with a finer tip, deviating from the stylus of greater mass used for 78s. To accommodate this need for precision, sapphires and diamonds were employed for stylus tips. A noteworthy diamond-tip cartridge was made by London (formerly Decca), utilizing a unique L-shaped cantilever constructed on nonmagnetic steel. Prior to the 1950s, the stylus was based on a piezoelectric ceramic material. While ceramic continued to be used into the 1950s, the momentum shifted to smaller, lighter, and more compliant magnetic cartridges. These new cartridges diminished record wear and created better sound, finding favor among audiophiles and eventually becoming the standard-bearer of cartridge design for generations to come.

Tonearm design of the 1950s was likewise not immune to critical changes. The older arms used to play 78s were extremely heavy, as a bulky mass was required for an electric cartridge to track on a shellac disc. As companies such as Fairchild, General Electric, Ortofon, Pickering, and Shure introduced newer moving-coil cartridges, tonearms required less mass in their construction. As a result, brands such as Ortofon and SME began to produce arms of much lighter weight, another trend that would continue into current tonearm design. On the more exotic side of 1950s tonearm method were linear-tracking arms. The idea was to create a tangential tonearm that could track a record's grooves in the same linear manner in which they were laterally cut. An early 1950s company called Ortho-Sonic created a tangential arm in which the cartridge would slide across the record by way of ball bearings, diminishing friction while preserving the inertia needed to track the groove. The merits of this method would not fade by the end of the 1950s, finding support in subsequent tangential arms, notably developed by Bang & Olufsen (B&O), Clearaudio, Goldmund, Pierre Lurné, Rabco, Revox, and Souther.

○○   The Birth of the Microgroove LP

As early as 1931, RCA Victor attempted to introduce a long-playing 33⅓-rpm record, along with an expensive new player to accommodate these new LPs, but the market was unimpressed. After all, the recordings were just poorly conceived transfers from the original four-minute-long shellac pressings, which yielded consistently poor fidelity. The inappropriate Depression-era timing for the release of new records that required expensive machines for playback sealed the fate of RCA Victor's LP endeavor.

At the time the conventional thinking was that a record could only be made to play longer in two ways: by slowing down the speed of revolutions or by reducing the space between the grooves, thereby maximizing the number of grooves. Achieving slower speeds through precariously tight grooves posed daunting technical obstacles that baffled engineers for three decades.

Prepared to overcome these hurdles, in 1944 Columbia set up an ad hoc laboratory headed by Peter Goldmark, a gifted Hungarian immigrant. (Goldmark's later work in color-television technology cemented his standing in the scientific community: President Jimmy Carter awarded him the National Medal of Science "for contributions to the development of the communication sciences for education, entertainment, culture, and human service."[51]) The unmistakable proof of Goldmark's efforts for Columbia was laid bare in his development of the microgroove record. By 1947 he created a recording head that had the ability to cut tapered and closely aligned grooves (measuring 0.003 inches or 0.007 centimeters), a cartridge that would track these grooves, and a brilliant equalization system to address the challenges of poor sound from the inside grooves. The new record had between 224 and 226 grooves per inch; formerly records held 80 to 100 grooves per inch.[52] In designing the new discs, Goldmark moved away from heavy shellac to a lighter material, vinyl, and changed the revolutions per minute from 78 to 33⅓.[53] Playing back the microgroove records with his new lightweight cartridge produced a greatly improved fidelity of sound.[54]

Eager to demonstrate Goldmark's efforts, Columbia corralled the press for a demonstration at the Waldorf Astoria hotel in New York City. The year was 1948, and many of the journalists present had also witnessed Victor's failed introduction of its LP technology in 1931; enthusiasm was rather muted, and expectations were quite low. This would quickly change as Columbia's president, Edward Wallerstein, persuasively demonstrated the merits of the Goldmark LP. Towering on one side of him was an 8-foot (2.4-meter) stack of conventional shellac discs, and on his other side was a comparatively Lilliputian 15-inch (38.1-centimeter) stack of the new microgroove LPs: both stacks contained the same amount of music. Wallerstein cleverly played a four-minute-long 78, and at the format's usual interruption for changing discs, he transitioned to playing a new LP of the same music with its uninterrupted playing time of twenty-three minutes.

The LP was able not only to play for a longer duration, present less surface noise, and diminish disc wear but also to reduce the amount of physical space required for storage. Naturally, consumers were enticed by the monetary savings as well, since a single LP could be purchased for less money than the five 78s that were musically equivalent.

Efficiency wasn't the only determinant in the LP's rise; for certain, the sonic fidelity of LPs was greatly improved over that of 78s. The key detriment in the sound produced by shellac was how it was recorded, by way of a direct recording on wax or acetate blanks. The long-playing record, however, was able to take full advantage of the new tape-recording technology and its rapid ubiquity in recording studios. Recording within a range of twenty to twenty thousand cycles, tape offered a tremendous advancement in improved sound.

In addition, it could record continuously for more than thirty minutes, leaving musicians free to perform without taking the frequent breaks that were required to accommodate the more limited, older technology. Further, with an unprecedented allowance for editing, the recording could be transferred to the microgroove master in a more artistically complete form. Arturo Toscanini, Leopold Stokowski, and Bing Crosby served as early and notable advocates of recording on tape.[55]

Armed with the new LPs, Columbia needed a record player to play them and enlisted Philco, a Philadelphia-based firm, to build the required turntables, tonearms, and pickups. As opposed to a traditional console-based system with integrated record player, amplifier, and speakers, Philco's approach created the blueprint for, and ushered in, the era of the standalone turntable.

○○   Battle of the Speeds

Two months prior to the launch of the long-playing record at the Waldorf Astoria, Columbia's executives decided to introduce the new disc's glories to RCA Victor, its long-standing rival. The motivation was to collectively and convincingly switch the preference of the industry to the new format. Initially there was reason to be optimistic as David Sarnoff, RCA's president at the time, spoke highly of the new 33⅓-rpm LP. Surprisingly, and contrary to the inaugural enthusiasm, Columbia's executives did not hear back from RCA Victor and decided to go it alone.[56]

RCA Victor was not immune to the appeal of the revolutionary LP, but the proud Eldridge Johnson at the helm was reluctant to take a back seat to Columbia. With the efforts of RCA Victor's engineers, the company's rebuttal to Columbia materialized in the form of a microgroove record in the guise of a seven-inch 45-rpm Vinylite disc. In order to accommodate its new 45s, RCA Victor released what it called the "world's fastest record changer," with its 9JY and 9EY3 players, implicitly pursuing a convenience-based, mass-market approach, leaving the more discerning market (namely that for classical music) to Columbia.[57] The record changer was designed to address the shorter playing time of a 45 and the necessary breaks between playing discs as compared to an LP. Offering nonstop playback by way of a stack of records that would sequentially drop onto a turntable was RCA Victor's counteroffensive to the Columbia LP.[58]

The LP's charms, however, were increasingly difficult to resist as Columbia facilitated the new format's broader acceptance by extending rights to record labels eager to adopt it. Quick to sign on were Mercury, Decca, London (Decca's export label), Concert Hall, Vox, and Cetra-Soria.[59] One early notable holdout was the England-based EMI, which lost almost four million dollars by the time it finally relented.[60]

In January 1950, with its prestige and honor significantly dulled, RCA Victor adopted the LP, introducing its "great artists and unsurpassed classical library on new and improved Long Play (33⅓) records."[61] RCA's capitulation to the LP was by no means a eulogy for 45s, as it began to successfully penetrate a new market for popular (that is, nonclassical) music. The smaller, unbreakable 45-rpm record found ample appeal among fans, who discovered its convenience and broader repertoire. This younger audience was also attracted to the mushrooming musical talent of the period. In this regard, the 45-rpm record can also be lauded for bringing rock and roll to the masses.[62]

○○   The Birth of High Fidelity and the Modern Turntable

It is no understatement that the LP ushered in the age of high fidelity, a term generously used by 1950s marketing teams. With the LP's promise of wider dynamic range, lower noise, longer playing time, and greater sonic fidelity, a phenomenon in audio manufacturing resulted. In the marketplace, a newfound obsession with high-fidelity separate components took root, with audio fairs demonstrating a fecund display of merchandise. The first notable show was the New York Audio Fair in 1949, serving voracious interests in audio reproduction.[63]

During this period, referred to as the golden age of the audio industry, new magazines such as *High Fidelity* exposed consumers to the latest equipment as well as news from the musical and recording world.[64] Hi-fi hobbyists were also part of a new DIY movement that espoused building one's own components, planting the seeds for turntable designers decades later.

With the advent of the LP, the curtain descended on 78s, shellac, and the surprisingly enduring phonograph. By the 1950s Edison's talking machines, along with their vertically cut cylinders, had become objects in museum exhibits. To interpret this as Edison's ultimate concession would distort history and dishonor his legacy. In truth, Edison succeeded in what he set out to do, with the evolution of his intent eventually fulfilled: "In the far-off future, when our descendants wish to conjure our simple little Wagner operas with the complex productions of their days, requiring, perhaps a dozen orchestras playing in half-a-dozen keys at once, they will have an accurate phonographic record of our harmonic simplicity."[65]

◯◯ A. R. Sugden & Co.

In the early 1950s Arnold Sugden, a self-taught engineer with no formal training in electronics, founded his eponymous company. By 1953 Sugden began designing turntables, tonearms, and cartridges for his Connoisseur line. Remarkably, he built his own cutting lathe in order to manufacture early microgroove LPs, which were intended to be played back on his turntables. While lacking the historical accolades of Alan Blumlein in the narrative of early stereo, Sugden was in many respects the most impressive pioneer in turntable stereo reproduction. Prior to the industrial embrace of stereo, he developed early stereo cartridges, lower-mass tonearms to accommodate the new cartridges, and belt-drive turntables, which later became the dominant drive system in contemporary tables.

1.1	CONNOISSEUR TURNTABLE, A. R. SUGDEN, 1950s

1.1

○○ Birmingham Sound Reproducers (BSR)

Daniel McLean McDonald established Birmingham Sound Reproducers in Great Britain in 1932. By 1951 the company became prominent in designing and manufacturing automatic and manual turntables as well as changers for record players. BSR supplied changers for the popular Dansette brand of record players, helping Dansette become a highly recognized brand in the United Kingdom. By the early 1960s, BSR also assisted B&O in developing its tape-deck technology, a testament to BSR's range of analog skills and contributions.

1.2   MONARCH RECORD PLAYER, BSR, 1950s

1.2

○○ Braun

Dieter Rams's post–World War II vision of a brave new world endowed Braun turntable designs with a distinctive German Modernist quality. The Braun company strongly advocated teamwork in the design process, and its turntables were collaborative efforts, with notables such as Gerd A. Müller, Hans Gugelot, and the team at Werkstatt Wagenfeld. The 1950s would showcase Braun's most iconic record player, the SK 4. Famously called "Snow White's Coffin," it laid the groundwork for 1950s mid-century turntable designs. The combination of lacquered sheet steel, elm, acrylic, and a Plexiglas dust cover garnered a laudatory response from design circles, most notably appearing in New York's Museum of Modern Art from 1958 to 1959. Rams's functionalist creed additionally found its way into his dedicated turntable, namely the PC 3, and into the P 1 of 1959, perhaps the most iconic portable record player ever made. Its design characteristics would later imbue his Atelier line of audio products, which later firms such as T+A and ADS adopted in their designs.

1.3

1.4

1.5

1.6

1.7

1.8

○○   Collaro

Christopher Collaro, a Greek national who immigrated to England in his early teens, founded his eponymous company in 1920. Soon after its establishment, Collaro quickly became a formidable entity in the manufacture of gramophone spring motors, supplying the industry with products described in its advertisements as "strong, silent, compact, and British."[66] After World War II, Collaro shifted to producing primarily record changers in addition to its own brand of record players. Awarded multiple patents, Collaro would eventually become one of the world's largest suppliers of record changers in the 1950s and 1960s.

| 1.9 | 4T200 RECORD PLAYER, COLLARO, 1950s |

1.9

○○   Decca

Although more prominent as a record label than as an audio manufacturer, Decca contributed meaningfully to analog record replay. Having worked during World War II with the British military on a technology to distinguish British from German submarines, Decca created its full-frequency-range recording (FFRR) system and began marketing the first FFRR discs after the war. On the heels of its newly released FFRR record production, Decca introduced the Decca London cartridge in addition to the Decca International tonearm. Its unique cartridge featured fixed coils and magnets and an L-shaped cantilever that terminated in a diamond stylus tip. The tonearm was sui generis as well, with a silicone-fluid-damped unipivot design, using magnetic force to support the arm and featuring anti-skate adjustment. These features would find their way into myriad future tonearm designs.

1.10   DP910 PORTABLE RECORD PLAYER, DECCA, 1950s

1.10

○○ Dansette

Another popular English brand was Dansette, manufactured by J & A Margolin, a London-based firm. Commencing sales of its record players in the early 1950s, Dansette sold at least one million players by the 1960s. Acclaimed for their versatility, the machines were capable of playing seven-, ten-, and twelve-inch records at up to four speeds, accommodating multiple generations of record formats, and machines were often equipped with BSR autochangers, permitting multiple-record playback. Emphasizing portability, the period's Viva, Junior, Monarch, and Diplomat models served the company well. Dansette's early Plus-a-Gram and Senior players were quite expensive, but teenagers eventually began acquiring them due to the brand's fashionable image. Appealing to the younger demographic, Dansette marketed its Junior De Luxe models to adolescents with great success.

1.11   POPULAR PORTABLE RECORD PLAYER, DANSETTE, 1962

1.11

1.12

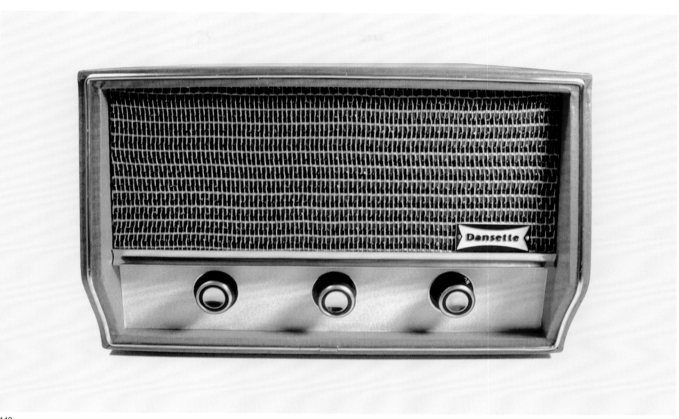

1.13

1.14

○○   Elektromesstechnik (EMT)

Few turntables are revered as much as—or have a more enduring following than—EMT designs. Wilhelm Franz founded the company as Elektromesstechnik Wilhelm Franz K. G. in Berlin in 1938. After the war, he envisioned a turntable range built to higher and more durable broadcasting standards. Collaborating with the Rundfunktechnisches Institut ("broadcasting technique institute"), EMT released its legendary 927 turntable in 1951. Implementing a massive platter with a Papst motor-driven idler wheel, the robust, tanklike build served as a catalyst for many turntables still in use today. The slightly more economical 930 model followed, and 1958 ushered in stereo versions of the 927 and 930 models. EMT sought Ortofon's help for its first tonearm, the RF-297, along with a magnetic cartridge designed for EMT. Housing its own proprietary phono preamplifier, the original monaural version would go through revisions as stereo became prevalent by the late 1950s. With austere Bakelite plinths combined with steel open frames, EMT turntables earned a consistently exacting reputation for rigorous quality.

| 1.15 | 927 TURNTABLE, EMT, 1951 (THIS MODEL, 1953) |
| 1.16 | 927A TURNTABLE, EMT, 1954 |

1.15

1.16

○○   Fairchild

Founded by Sherman Fairchild, this company was based in the United States, developing products for both professional and consumer markets. Fairchild came on the 1950s scene with an emphasis on cutting lathes for the recording industry and high-quality devices for domestic playback. The compact and lightweight 225 moving-coil cartridge, along with the 412 turntable and 280A tonearm, drew support within audiophile circles. Although expensive for its time, the 412 turntable was especially notable for its early electrical oscillator, which provided nonmechanical control of the platter speed. In addition, it had the option of being powered by a battery, a method used decades later by Simon Yorke and Thales turntable designs.

1.17   412 TURNTABLE, FAIRCHILD, 1950s

1.17

○○ Philco

The introduction of the microgroove LP required a turntable to play it. Naturally a symbiotic relationship arose between a record label and a turntable manufacturer. In this case, Columbia enlisted Philco to build the first machines capable of playing the new discs. Philco quickly introduced its M-15 model, which only played at 33⅓ rpm, was constructed in Bakelite, was designed to play seven-, ten-, and twelve-inch records, and featured a mechanism for automatic start and stop. The M-15 was referred to as a "record player attachment," an early description for a component that required an amplifier, phono preamplifier, and speaker.[67] This novel concept of separate components was eventually embraced by hi-fi culture. Compared to its competitors, Philco was quite technologically advanced. In 1955 Philco introduced the world's first all-transistor turntables, the TPA-1 and TPA-2, displacing vacuum tubes and using D batteries as the power supply. As portable designs, they garnered much attention from the marketplace. But by 1956 Philco ceased production, as the cost of transistors was prohibitive compared to that of thermionic predecessors.

1.18   M-15 RECORD PLAYER, PHILCO, 1948

1.18

○○   Garrard

Within the hierarchy of 1950s turntables, Garrard's lofty ranking is nei-ther hyperbole nor based on vintage turntable romanticism. The company's legacy dates from its inception in 1735. Founded by the silversmith George Wickes, Garrard was appointed as the first official crown jeweller of the United Kingdom and was responsible for the upkeep of the crown jewels. In 1915 Garrard and Company was established and transitioned to manufacturing parts for the military, subsequently shifting to making spring-wound gram-ophone motors for companies such as Columbia and Decca. By the 1950s all efforts were focused on building an extremely high-end transcription turntable. The result was the Garrard 301, released in 1954. Able to play 33⅓-, 45-, and 78-rpm records, it featured an imposing and enormous motor that drove an idler, rotating the platter by its rim. The base was constructed of alumi-num and finished first in gray and later in off-white. Garrard initially made it avail-able with grease bearings but switched to oil bearings in 1957. Similar to models by EMT and the Thorens TD 124, the Garrard 301 maintains a deservedly prom-inent status. Lovingly collected and painstakingly restored, the 301 serves as a key emissary for 1950s turntable designs.

1.19   301 STATEMENT TURNTABLE, GARRARD, RESTORED AND UPGRADED BY ARTISAN FIDELITY, 2018

1.19

○○   Lenco

The name of this company is derived from the surname of its creators, Fritz and Marie Laeng, an ambitious couple who desired to create fine audio products in Burgdorf, Switzerland. Established in 1946, Lenco became known for its durable idler-drive turntables, namely their F50 and B50-16 models, which were introduced in the 1950s. The F50 went through various iterations in the 1950s, ranging from a three-speed to a four-speed with a fixed tonearm; by the late 1950s, the F50 was updated with a removable Bakelite headshell. Spartan yet dependable, the F50 nevertheless became dormant within the annals of audio design. Recently, however, Lenco tables have been unearthed by analog circles, and enthusiasts are seeking out prime examples for bespoke restorations.

1.20   F50-8 TURNTABLE, LENCO, 1948 (THIS MODEL, 1955)

1.20

○○ Grundig

Antithetical to the Modernist movement of the 1950s, some firms continued to manufacture large consoles that housed turntables, tape recorders, and radios. The console form remained popular into the 1950s, and the German-based Grundig produced some of the period's finest examples. The company's popular Majestic console was available in a multitude of variations and was sold by an exclusive network of dealers. The turntable often used by Grundig was sourced from Perpetuum Ebner, a long-standing record-player manufacturer in Germany.

1.21–23 MAJESTIC 9070 STEREO CONSOLE, GRUNDIG, 1956 [BELOW AND OVERLEAF, LEFT AND RIGHT]

1.21

○○ Philips

Often descriptions of 1950s turntable designs tend to emphasize the industrial and broadcast motives of the period. Philips, however, took a counterintuitive and more whimsical approach. This was unusual because Philips, the Dutch powerhouse of electronic-goods manufacturing, had the resources to build turntables at the level of EMT, Garrard, or Thorens but instead chose to design and market colorful and lively portables. Like the charming Dansette or fashionable Decca, Philips wanted to appeal to a younger postwar generation. In the early 1950s, Philips released a series of portable players, beginning with the 22GP200, which combined leather and plastic and played 33⅓ LPs along with 45s. Following these with the Sentinel multicolor lineup, Philips became a leader in commercial record-player branding, and its products became known as players for the masses.

1.24	SENTINEL PORTABLE RECORD PLAYER, PHILIPS, 1950s
1.25	PHONOKOFFER III RECORD PLAYER, PHILIPS, 1953 [OPPOSITE]

1.24

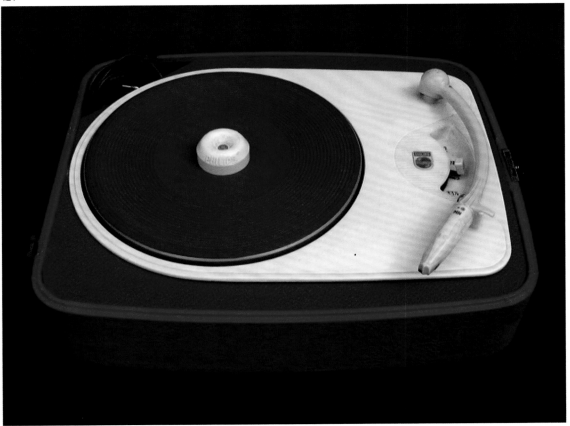

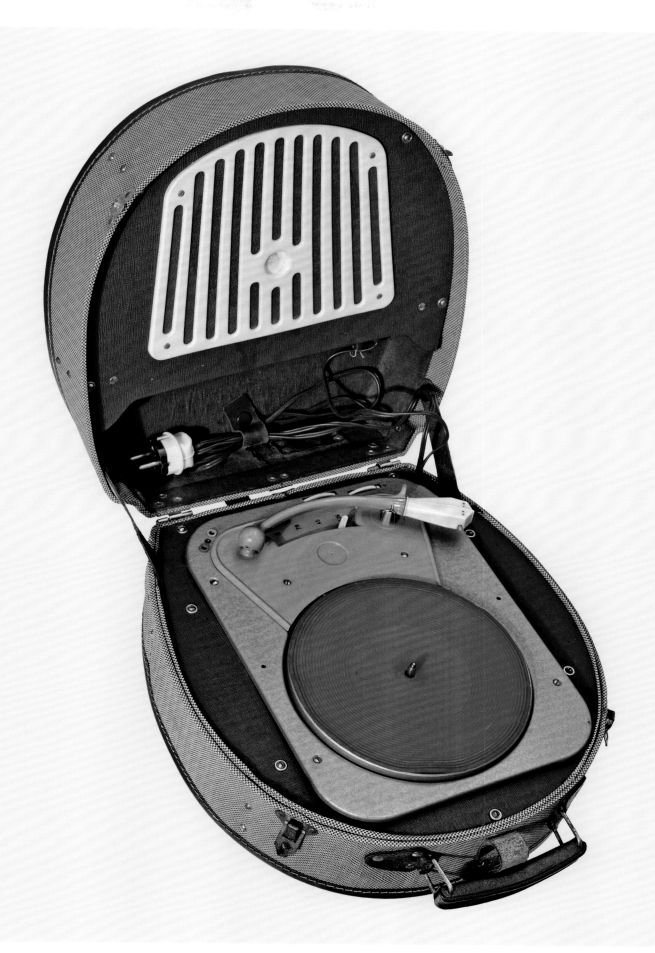

○○ RCA Victor

RCA Victor's early shunning of Columbia's microgroove LP, and pursuit of its 45-rpm record, led to a movement in smaller and daintier players and record changers. RCA Victor embarked on a marketing campaign proclaiming the 45's superiority over Columbia's LP, claiming that "Toscanini, Koussevitzky, Rubinstein, Heifetz, Horowitz, and many other great music authorities listened to the '45' and pronounced it the finest of all recorded music."[68] Its first player to enter the market was the RCA Victor 45, which could be used as a complete automatic player or as an attachment. The auto-changer could play a maximum of ten records and up to fifty minutes of music. RCA Victor ultimately adopted Columbia's microgroove LP, but the 45 would live on into the 1980s. What did not survive was enthusiasm for stand-alone 45-rpm disc players; most post-1950s turntables accommodated both speeds and formats.

1.26   9-EY-3 PHONOGRAPH, RCA VICTOR, c.1949

1.26

○○ Rek-O-Kut

This brand's name originates from when it made lathes called recorders or disc-cutting machines. Rek-O-Kut was an industry standard for many 1950s broadcast studios and radio stations and was famous for its diverse range in drive mechanisms. The company's three-speed idler-and-rim-drive B-16H transcription table from 1949 established its reputation for making machines that were bulletproof workhorses. Built from cast aluminum that was radial ribbed for solidity and featuring a massive 15-inch (38.1-centimeter) platter, the B-16H rivaled the EMT tables of the day. With the subsequent LP-743 and popular Rondine models of the mid-1950s, Rek-O-Kut proved it could shoulder the standard for broadcast transcription tables.

1.27   T-12H EXCLUSIVE TURNTABLE, REK-O-KUT, REPRODUCED AND UPGRADED BY TORQUEO AUDIO, c.2016

1.27

○○ Leak

Another distinguished entity from the English school of audio designers was founded by Harold Joseph Leak in 1934. The company established itself in the 1950s for its amplifiers and speakers, but its dynamic pickup and tonearm and its stereo pickup were impressive contributions as well. Five years of research and development resulted in a tonearm with extremely low inertia, in which friction was reduced by a single pivot bearing. Providing its own step-up transformer for its diamond-stylus pickup, Leak comprehensively addressed the turntable's front end.

○○ Burne Jones

While the analog culture of the 1950s certainly brought more prominence to turntable design, tonearm innovation picked up later in the decade in order to accommodate stereo cartridges. One of the more exotic exceptions to this general rule was the Burne Jones Super 90 tangential arm. The objective of a tangential arm is to track the grooves of a record in a continuous radial line, tracing the groove just as it was cut. At the time conventional tonearm design favored pivoted arms that cross over a record's surface from a single pivot point. With fewer parts and less complexity than tangential arms, pivoted arms were cheaper to build, but theoretically they tracked poorly due to the offset cartridge's inability to remain tangential to the record surface, especially as it neared the grooves closest to the center of the disc. Espousing a straight-line-tracking methodology, Burne Jones in the 1950s was an early pioneer of the more complex and puristic tangential arms. Although the pivoted arm continued to be the dominant type of tonearm for decades, many later high-end designers built upon the Burne Jones foundation with state-of-the-art tangential arms.

1.28	DIAMOND LP PICKUP, LEAK, 1950s
1.29	SUPER 90 TANGENTIAL TONEARM, BURNE JONES, 1950s

1.28

1.29

○○ Ortofon

Very few analog manufacturing firms can compete with Ortofon's legacy and current relevance in the ongoing analog revival. The venerable Danish company dates from 1918, when it was founded by Arnold Poulsen and Axel Petersen. During its early days, Ortofon invested heavily in moving-coil magnetic technology for films, later applying what it learned from that industry to building machines for record playback. By the 1950s the company could boast various designs such as the AB, A, and C monophonic moving-coil pickups. The C-type was made with professional broadcast tracking requirements in mind, and its stylus is the same unit as Ortofon's current SPU CG 25. So respected were Ortofon's moving-coil designs that EMT selected one for its 927 turntable along with the Ortofon-designed RF-297 tonearm (as mentioned earlier in the section on EMT), later replaced by the RF-229. Both tonearms were designed to accommodate the A and C cartridges. Ortofon-branded versions were the SMG-212 and RF-309. By 1957 Ortofon demonstrated its range of skills by introducing a stereo cutter head. Continuing the company's advancements in stereo replay, its famed engineer, Robert Gudmandsen, designed the stereo pickup, popularly referred to as the SPU. This device followed the configuration of the Neumann DST-62 head, with an extra set of contacts arranged at right angles. Today SPUs continue to be produced by Ortofon and are a popular and synergistic choice for restored vintage tables.

| 1.30 | PU C DIAMOND C-TYPE CARTRIDGE, ORTOFON, 1950s |
| 1.31 | RM-309 TONEARM, ORTOFON, 1950s |

1.30

1.31

1960s

○○   A Culmination of Turntable Mechanisms:
Idler Drive, Belt Drive, Direct Drive

The trends of the 1950s exemplified consumers' preference for convenience. Record changers dominated the turntable scene, and such utility dictated the type of mechanism needed. With the heavy weight of multiple records stacked on a spindle, a powerful drive system with tremendous torque was required in order to rotate records at correct speeds.

To achieve this, the favored mechanism was the idler drive, in which a motor-driven rubber wheel sits underneath the platter. This design isolates the idler wheel to prevent the vibrations created by the motor from resonating through the platter. However, the idler wheel is still coupled to the motor and, due to the high torque requirements, higher vibrations are inevitable. This challenge certainly did not prevent the German company Dual from refining the idler-drive mechanism in its popular 1009 and 1019 tables of the 1960s. Yet it was clear that the industry was transitioning away from the idler drive.

In an effort to keep the platter vibration-free, an efficient belt-drive mechanism was introduced in the 1960s, which greatly simplified matters. Implementing a smaller and less powerful motor, which spun a rubber belt that was wrapped around the platter, the belt-drive mechanism had an isolated motor and was believed to absorb vibrations. One notable belt-drive table was built by Acoustic Research, which introduced three-point suspension and spearheaded the belt-drive movement. By the 1970s even Dual, with its emphasis on idler-drive execution, eventually expanded its product line to include belt-drive tables, acknowledging the benefits of this mechanism while addressing market demand.

Perhaps even more remarkable in terms of mechanism evolution—and culturally pervasive in the history of turntable design—was the invention of the direct-drive turntable. The brainchild of Shuichi Obata, an engineer for Technics, a brand of Matsushita (which became Panasonic), this mechanism implements a motor located under the platter, directly coupled to and spinning the bearing upon which the platter is placed. Avoiding problems of wear and tear on the belt and slow start-up times, direct-drive tables were initially aimed at the professional sector, with Obata's 1969 introduction of the legendary SP-10.[69] Expanding into the consumer market with the later SL-1100 and SL-1200 models, Technics turntables would eventually find permanent residence in DJ circles beginning in the 1970s and continuing through the 2000s.[70] Through its design innovation, Technics would help usher in a wave of myriad Japanese turntables in the 1970s and 1980s, as discussed in greater depth in chapter 4.

○○   From Mono to Stereo

The development of various drives and the growing market for turntables and vinyl discs were propelled by a fundamental element in analog culture: the desire for stereo sound recording and playback. As described by Hans Fantel: "Stereo was invented millions of years ago when two-eyed, two-eared creatures first appeared on earth. You perceive the world in pairs with your two eyes and two ears. That's what makes your sense of sight and sound three-dimensional."[71]

By the late 1950s, the intuitive understanding of stereo was nothing new. Even much earlier, by 1881, a practical application of stereo had occurred in Paris: Clément Ader, a French engineer, had an idea to place telephone transmitters onstage and to broadcast performances to subscribers listening at home. As the New York Times quoted from Ader's patent: "'The transmitters (i.e., telephone mouthpieces) are distributed in two groups on the stage—a left and right one. The subscriber has likewise two receivers, one of them connected to the left ground of transmitters, the other to the right one… This double listening to sound, received and transmitted by two different sets of apparatus, produces the same effect on the ear that the stereoscope produces on the eye.' In short, Ader had invented stereophonic sound reproduction."[72]

While this nineteenth-century acknowledgment of stereo reproduction occurred, the concept's development would have to wait until the 1930s. Alan Blumlein, a senior engineer at EMI's Central Research Laboratories, had reportedly been frustrated at the cinema after hearing the film's sound from a distant single speaker. Blumlein rejected a simplistic application of stereo that required only two speakers corresponding to two ears, instead focusing on re-creating the acoustic space and on retaining the elements of spatial factors in reproducing music. He succeeded in cutting a disc with two grooves that could be traced and played back concurrently and in concert. His research led him to develop a needle that could retrieve two signals from a specially cut groove, effectively resulting in stereo reproduction. Creatively combining the antiquated hill-and-dale method espoused by Thomas Edison and the lateral technique championed by Emile Berliner, he success-fully put two separate channels within the same groove. Blumlein applied in 1931 for a patent in "binaural sound," and he can be credited as the father of modern stereo reproduction.[73]

Following on the heels of Blumlein's achievement, the conductor Leopold Stokowski, with support from Bell Labs, explored stereo reproduc-tion in the musical arts, manifesting commercially in the Fantasound stereo system for Walt Disney's animated film, *Fantasia*.[74] But curiously Bell Labs was reluctant to further such efforts, and by the 1950s the status of stereo had descended, becoming nugatory and inconsequential. Perhaps this was due to the practical difficulties in making a stereo record. Despite this period of malaise, a few noteworthy entities espoused stereo replay and pushed forward with the medium.

One such entity was Cook Records, founded by Emory Cook. In 1952 Cook was the first to produce commercial stereo records, referring to them as "binaural." He achieved this by cutting two independent mono tracks that required two separate cartridges, carefully aligned, to achieve binaural play-back. To this end, he created what he called a binaural clip-on, which would attach to a preexisting tonearm and hold a second cartridge.[75]

Also joining these early efforts in stereo was Arnold Sugden, of the Connoisseur line of turntables and tonearms, who demonstrated a two-channel single-groove record. His method was utilized on a somewhat grander scale by the record labels Decca in England and Telefunken in Germany.[76] In 1954 engineers at RCA Victor also contributed toward research in stereo reproduction, along with Robert Fine at Mercury and Tom Dowd at Atlantic, all independently striving for a common goal.[77] Despite these pio-neering efforts, however, the commercial viability of stereo reproduction remained illusory and aspirational at best.

OO   From Magnetic Tape to Stereo Records

The birth of stereo records could not develop without the contem-poraneous advancements of magnetic-tape technology. Although AEG in Germany was at the forefront in the development of magnetic tape, it was an American soldier's efforts that allowed this technology to find its way into the recording and playback industry. At the end of World War II, Jack Mullin, an Army Signal Corps engineer, was sent to Germany to retrieve and assess captured electrical equipment. One of his finds was AEG's Magnetophon, used extensively by the Nazis for recording and broadcasting purposes. On May 16, 1946, after disassembling and extensively modifying the Magnetophon, Mullin presented it to the Institute of Radio Engineers in San Francisco. Many in the audience that day would later work for Ampex, the pioneering magnetic-tape company.[78]

Based on what the engineers heard, and borrowing generously from the Magnetophon, Ampex invested heavily in tape technology, resulting in its first Model 200 tape recorder, released in 1952. The Model 200 was a single-track (mono) machine, but Ampex was resolute in building two-track (stereo) machines. However, the executives understood that it only made sense to pursue the manufacturing of two-track machines if the recording industry embraced two-track and two-channel recordings as well. At the 1953 New York Audio Fair, Ross Snyder of Ampex, along with Bill Cara, a recording buff and audio salesman, presented a multitrack recording they had made. Recorded at the train station, it captured high-decibel sounds of trains approaching and leaving the platform along with other sounds, such as steam blowing. Re-created through a newly developed Ampex 400 multitrack machine, the recording played back the aural fireworks through three widely spaced speakers at the audio fair, convincing and impressing the attendees.[79]

With this reinvigorated and renewed interest, stereo recordings found their way onto tape, which consumers could play back on the new, but pricey, Ampex machines. By the late 1950s, the major labels were already contemplating how to universally transition to stereo records without repeating the speed wars that took place earlier in the decade. The industry needed to adopt a standard of stereo LP pressing that would allow the market to securely embrace the new medium. This objective was met by the cutting system by Westrex, a Western Electric subsidiary. During the period of magnetic tape's popularity, Westrex was discreetly developing a new stereo cutter that would replace its dated monaural designs. On August 26, 1957, Westrex invited the industry's leading engineering representatives to a demonstration in its Hollywood laboratory. Capitol Records supplied the source material: its tape to Westrex's stereo-cut disc called "Introduction to Stereo."

While it was neither the role nor purpose of the attendees to determine the stereo-cutting standard for the industry, the collective enthusiasm for the Westrex demonstration led to the adoption of the Westrex 45/45 system by the Recording Industry Association of America (RIAA) on December 27, 1957.[80] The RIAA was the first trade association of record labels in the United States, and its purpose was to set standards for the recording industry. Its first notable accomplishment is believed to have taken place in 1954, when it set a standard equalization curve for recording and playback of vinyl records.[81] But the RIAA's more significant embrace of the Westrex stereo format laid the foundation for all turntable, tonearm, and cartridge design methods as the industry moved into the 1960s, the first decade of stereo.

○○   Acoustic Research (AR)

Founded by two audio visionaries, Edgar Villchur and Henry Kloss, AR became famous for its invention of the acoustic suspension speaker. Following this success, AR applied its know-how to turntable design, releasing the revolutionary XA turntable in 1961. On display at the Museum of Modern Art for its contribution to industrial design, the XA turntable established the blueprint for most subsequent designs. Isolation was achieved by placing the tonearm and platter on a sub-platform, which was suspended underneath a top plate at three points using damped springs. This method was notable for its ability to shelter the turntable from exterior vibrations, such as footfalls or acoustic feedback. An early advocate of the belt-drive mechanism, AR refined its approach with a lightweight platter (similar to the path of Acoustical) and a low-power motor mounted to the upper plate, not the sub-platform, thus keeping motor vibrations away from the record and the sensitive cartridge. Achieving an impressively low degree of rumble and accurate belt-driven speed, the XA was noted by other companies, most famously evidenced in the Thorens TD 150 and Linn Sondek LP12.

2.1   XA TURNTABLE, ACOUSTIC RESEARCH (WITH RB250 TONEARM, REGA), 1961

2.1

○○   Acoustical

Designed and manufactured in Holland, Acoustical began under the name Jobo, with an emphasis on broadcast-grade turntables. Throughout the 1960s, it produced the belt-driven 3100 turntable. As opposed to its many broadcast-turntable competitors, Acoustical opted for a lightweight platter made of particleboard in order to reduce rumble and avoid interference with the magnetic fields of the era's popular moving-coil cartridges. Driving the 3100's platter was the high-quality Papst Aussenläufer motor, with excellent start-up time and speed stability. The Jobo 2800 balanced tonearm utilized a spring to create downward force, achieving excellent tracking and serving as a popular companion to the 3100 turntable.

2.2–4   3100 TURNTABLE, ACOUSTICAL, c.1968

2.2

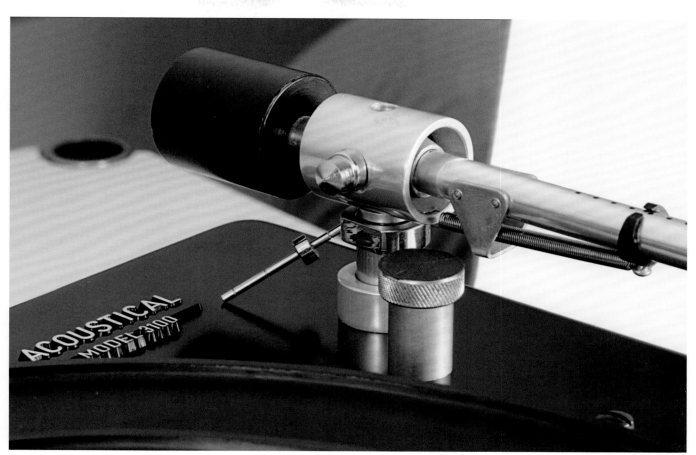

2.3

2.4

○○ Ariston

In the late 1960s and early 1970s, Scotland was a nerve center of turntable creativity. Leading the efforts was Hamish Robertson, who founded Ariston and commissioned Castle Precision Engineering to build the RD11 turntable. Ariston claimed it to be a simple design, but such modesty belies the table's sophistication. The 9½-pound (4.3-kilogram) platter was spun by an in-house-designed 24-pole synchronous motor, which reduced wow and flutter to an impressive 0.004 percent and lowered rumble to a praiseworthy 72 decibels. In an effort to reduce friction, the precision single-point main bearing rested on a ball bearing. Isolation was achieved using a shock-absorber system for the tonearm and platter. A slip-clutch feature further prevented belt deterioration. Since Castle was the company owned by Jack Tiefenbrun, whose son Ivor Tiefenbrun founded Linn shortly after the introduction of the RD11, any discussion of Ariston's roots invariably leads to the foundation provided for the Linn LP12 turntable introduced in the early 1970s.[82]

2.5   RD11S TURNTABLE, ARISTON (WITH SERIES III TONEARM, SME), 1970s

2.5

○○   Fairchild

Sherman Fairchild, a serial entrepreneur with a high degree of mechanical acumen, founded his namesake company, introducing recording devices for radio and broadcast applications in the 1950s and 1960s. The Fairchild 660 (mono) and 670 (stereo) limiters were used by the British Broadcasting Corporation, and Fairchild quickly became established in the professional-audio world, even building its own LP cutting lathe. With these skills, Fairchild resolutely introduced to the market an industrial broadcast turntable: the 4124. The structure was made of heavyweight steel, with two belts and a massive aluminum platter, and its hysteresis synchronous motor was isolated by way of dedicated vibration mounts. The speed of the table was controlled electronically, whereas most tables of the time were controlled mechanically. As a result, the 4124 was widely used in broadcast studios and is coveted by collectors to this day.

2.6   440 TURNTABLE, FAIRCHILD (WITH PRITCHARD TONEARM, AUDIO DYNAMICS CORPORATION), 1960

2.6

○○ Braun

Perpetuating its singular form factor into the 1960s, Braun now empha-sized significant engineering enhancements over the preceding decade's models of turntables. The introduction of stereo and a broader movement toward professional and broadcast tables incentivized Braun to update its range. The PS 2 was the last of the smaller, more lightweight Braun players that were popular in the 1950s. The company produced a larger plinth and platter and a reworked tonearm for its PCS 4 in 1961 and made more significant changes to the PS 500 of 1968, with a suspended platter on an injection-mold, solid-zinc sub-chassis with hydraulic damping. The Braun tracking force gauge precisely calculates the best balance for a stylus on a record player.

2.7	PCS 4 RECORD PLAYER, DIETER RAMS, BRAUN, 1961
2.8–9	PS2 RECORD PLAYER, DIETER RAMS, BRAUN, 1963

2.7

2.8

2.9

2.11

2.12

○○   Dual

Dating from 1927, this German company was aptly named for its pioneering dual-mode power supplies. By the 1960s Dual was an established turntable entity, but its 1965 introduction of the iconic 1019 model solidified its presence in the market. Dual became famous in the 1970s for offering the market a wide range of drive mechanisms, but the company preferred the idler drive in the 1960s and chose to implement it in the unusually high-torque 1019. Aficionados of 78-rpm discs are drawn to the 1019 for its high torque, and many examples are sought out for meticulous restoration.

2.13–16   1019 TURNTABLE, DUAL, 1965

2.13

2.14

2.15

2.16

○○ Electroacustic GmbH (ELAC)

Known also as Miracord, the German brand ELAC was quite popular in the 1960s, and its machines were aggressively distributed in the United States by the Benjamin Electronic Sound Corporation, which rebranded them with the name Benjamin Miracord. In 1957 ELAC patented an electromagnetic cartridge that immediately brought fame, enabling the company to globally license the cartridge design to audio entities, such as Shure. ELAC's technology also led to the development of moving-magnet (MM) cartridges. In the 1960s ELAC turned its attention to idler-drive tables, introducing, among others, the Miracord 10 and 10H studio series. The Miracord 10 had the flexibility to be used as a record changer, automatic turntable, manual turntable, or repeating turntable with four speeds. ELAC continues to this day, and the Miracord line of turntables was recently rereleased, attesting to the brand's legacy.

| 2.17 | BENJAMIN MIRACORD 10H TURNTABLE, ELAC, 1960s |
| 2.18 | MIRAPHON 12 PORTABLE RECORD PLAYER, ELAC, c.1959 [OPPOSITE] |

2.17

○○   Empire

Another contribution to the belt-drive wave in the 1960s was Herb Horowitz's Empire brand. Famous for its Troubador line of tables, the company's 398 turntable and 980 tonearm penetrated analog circles. Featuring an individually balanced platter and precision-honed bearing, the 398 was complemented with a Papst motor, which provided specifications of extremely low tolerances. Visually Empire turntables were quite attractive, with finishes offered in satin chrome, silver anodized aluminum, and anodized gold. The 980 tonearm was considerably high mass, with race ball bearings and a spring-balanced tonearm, resulting in accurate and smooth tracking.

2.19   TROUBADOR 398 TURNTABLE AND 980 TONEARM, EMPIRE, c.1963

2.20–21   TROUBADOR 598 II TURNTABLE AND 990 TONEARM, EMPIRE, 1972

2.19

2.20

2.21

○○ Garrard

Introduced in 1952, Garrard's 301 transcription table lasted an enviable twelve years before the company decided to better it with the 1964 release of the 401. The industrial designer Eric Marshall was enlisted by Garrard to design the 401 while maintaining the distinct industrial character of the 301. Mechanically the 401 deviated from the 301 with a newly designed platter, a new strobe, a more robust eddy current brake, and better placement of mains power cables. The 401 was similar to the 301 in terms of raw torque from a sizable motor along with a substantial bearing. Both the 301 and 401 have risen to the top of collector wish lists, with ambitious restoration efforts emanating from Shindo Labs in Japan and Artisan Fidelity in the United States.

2.22   401 TURNTABLE, GARRARD (WITH 3009 TONEARM, SME), 1965

2.23–24   401 STATEMENT TURNTABLE, GARRARD, RESTORED AND UPGRADED BY ARTISAN FIDELITY, 2018

2.22

2.23

2.24

○○   Transcriptors

It's one thing for a turntable to establish itself in audiophile or hobbyist circles and another thing for it to transcend geekdom to become a cultural icon of industrial design. The Transcriptors Hydraulic Reference turntable was featured in Stanley Kubrick's 1971 film, *A Clockwork Orange*. Kubrick selected the turntable to appear with the actor Malcolm McDowell (playing Alex), listening to Beethoven LPs.[83] Founded in 1960 by the iconoclast David Gammon, the UK-based company Transcriptors immediately drew acclaim for its futuristic and avant-garde designs, gifting a turntable in 1969 to the Museum of Modern Art in New York, which remains in the collection to this day. Transcriptors turntables were undeniably elegant in design but had substance as well: a lightweight tonearm, precision bearings, advanced motor isolation, and spring suspension all combined to offer excellent performance. The hydraulic element applies to a simple yet ingenious paddle hidden underneath the platter, bathed in silicone, and acting as a mechanism to slow down the speed. Grounding was accomplished via 24k gold-plated inertia platter weights, which created a unique and timeless design. Transcriptors designed its own unipivot tonearm, but its tables were often mated with SME arms, at customers' requests. In 1973, Transcriptors relocated to Carlow, Ireland, and David Gammon issued J. A. Michell the right to produce the Hydraulic Reference turntable under license, a contract that was terminated in November 1977. Transcriptors closed in 1981, though was reopened by David's son, Michael, in 2000.

2.25   HYDRAULIC REFERENCE TURNTABLE, DAVID GAMMON, TRANSCRIPTORS, 1964

2.25

○○   Teppaz

Not all 1960s turntables existed within the exclusive austerity of industrial and broadcasting designs. Countless manufacturers focused on whimsical and portable record players, which appealed to teenagers and people wanting music on the go. Companies in the 1950s began this tradition, but none did so as charmingly as Teppaz. Built in Craponne, in the district of Lyon, France, Teppaz became famous for its Oscar record player. With a combination of Modernist and Belle Époque styling, this portable French gem found immediate favor among a mainstream audience, eventually becoming a classic collector's item in design circles.

2.26   OSCAR PORTABLE RECORD PLAYER, TEPPAZ, 1963

2.26

2.27

2.28

2.29

2.30

○○   Thorens

Very few turntables can match the heritage and legacy of the venerable Thorens TD 124 (the initials "TD" stand for *tourne disque*, "record turner" in French). Establishing its primacy in the 1950s with the TD 124, Thorens decided by the mid-1960s to release the MKII version. The most important distinctions were: a more modern frame, a nonmagnetic engineered platter (allowing the use of a moving-coil cartridge), and a closer ring-patterned mat. Thorens further designed a new tonearm for the MKII, the TP14, which replaced the older BTD-12S arm. Compared favorably to the Garrard 301 and 401, the Thorens TD 124 MKII would join the top tier of classic turntable designs.[84] Even Bang & Olufsen borrowed the 124 for its own branded Beogram 3000 model. Today models of the TD 124 MKII are painstakingly restored by firms such as Swissonor and Schopper in Switzerland and Woodsong Audio in the United States.

2.31	BEOGRAM 3000 TURNTABLE, BANG & OLUFSEN (WITH TD124 MKII MOTOR UNIT, THORENS), 1967
2.32	TD 124 MKII TURNTABLE, THORENS (WITH RMG-212 TONEARM, ORTOFON), 1966
2.33	TD124 STATEMENT TURNTABLE, THORENS, RESTORED AND UPGRADED BY ARTISAN FIDELITY, 2017

2.31

2.32

2.33

○○ Grace

In Japan a school of precision tonearm craftsmanship developed quickly, and remarkable Japanese contributions to tonearm design cannot be overemphasized. One of the earliest examples to lead the pack was the Shinagawa Musen Company, with its Grace tonearm. Frequently witnessed on countless Garrard or Lenco tables of the day, Grace arms were prized due to their lightness, statically balanced character, and adjustable stylus pressure. A highly acclaimed 1960s model was the G-545, arguably the predecessor of many quality Japanese tonearms that followed.

2.34–35   G-545 TONEARM, GRACE, 1960s

2.34

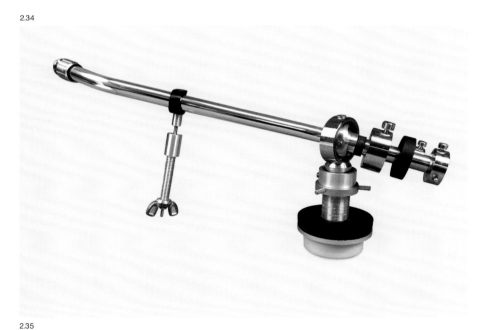

2.35

○○ Scale Model Equipment Company (SME)

Founded in 1946 by Alastair Robertson-Aikman, the Scale Model Equipment Company was initially unrelated to audio components, having been formed to engineer precision parts for scale models. Aikman decided to transition the company's efforts to building tonearms after venturing to build an arm for his own use. Beginning tonearm production in 1959 and changing its name to SME Limited, the company was able to build twenty-five tonearms per week, each of which was composed of individually crafted components. By the 1960s SME expanded production to the 3009 9-inch (22.3-centimeter) tonearm and 3012 12-inch (30.5-centimeter) tonearms, which were widely used by high-end audiophiles and the broadcast industry. Featuring a precision-machined steel tube with a lightweight headshell, anti-skating bias by way of a string, and high-tolerance horizontal bearings, the 3009 and 3012 became instant classics and industry standards for years to come. Future generations of SME arms would share characteristics with their 3009 and 3012 ancestors and would be produced in following decades.

2.36	3009 TONEARM, SME, 1960s
2.37	3012 TONEARM, SME, 1960s

2.36

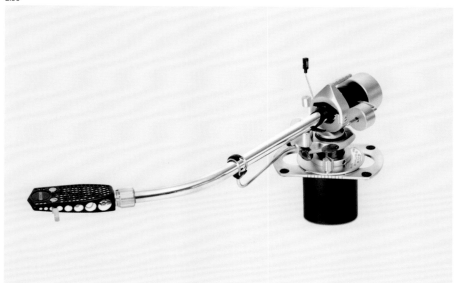

2.37

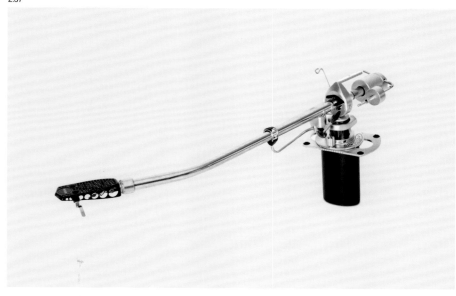

1970s

○○ Birth of the High-End Turntable and Tonearm

By the 1970s two turntable movements would take divergent courses and establish market themes for decades to come. On the one hand, a new movement had surfaced that elevated audio into a rarefied, expensive stratum. Deviating from the tanklike broadcast and professional tables of a decade earlier, models of the 1970s strayed from the industrial sensibilities of the past, favoring smaller yet technologically consolidated forms. Companies such as Audio Research, Dahlquist, Infiniti, Nakamichi, Mark Levinson, Quad, and Threshold effectively gave birth to a luxury segment in the audio component market. On the other hand, a counterdevelopment was emerging in Asia, spawning a multitude of mass-produced cheaper exports, flooding the global market, and making turntables accessible to most consumers.

Developing contemporaneously alongside the high-end electronics and speaker companies was a nascent and burgeoning turntable scene. One turntable led the pack and ushered in this era: Ivor Tiefenbrun's Linn Sondek LP12. Amazingly, the LP12 was neither sufficiently novel nor substantially revelatory in design to warrant placement at the helm of this movement. Quite similar to the Ariston RD11 (which Tiefenbrun's father manufactured at his engineering company), the Acoustic Research XA, and the Thorens TD 150, the Linn shared with these tables a spring-loaded suspended sub-chassis, wood plinth, and rubber-belt-driven platter. Where the Linn distinguished itself was in the precision machining of its single-point bearing, parts, and overall execution. This advantage naturally came from Tiefenbrun's access to his father's company and afforded Linn a decisive edge. Tiefenbrun guided Linn with the enthusiasm and conviction of a missionary, and the Linn acquired a cultish reputation with a loyal and devoted fan base that grew through the years. Despite the LP12's success, however, it was not without controversy, mostly stemming from its similarities with the aforementioned tables, in particular the Ariston. But over time, Linn shrugged off such criticism, and its LP12 became one of the most famous icons of turntable design, execution, and longevity.

While Asia in the 1970s favored mass-market turntable design, Japan's Micro Seiki elevated itself from the mainstream with products under its own brand while serving as an original equipment manufacturer for the Japanese brands Luxman, Denon, Sharp, Sansui, and others. Micro Seiki would catapult Japan into the high-end realm and help lead to the cutting-edge Nakamichi tables of the 1980s and state-of-the-art TechDAS tables of the 2000s. Denmark's Bang & Olufsen (B&O), having borrowed heavily from the Thorens TD 124 in the 1960s, finally emerged in the 1970s with its proprietary turntable designs, which allowed the company to establish itself as an eminent and sui generis audio-design firm. Espousing sophisticated hydraulic mechanisms, linear tracking arms, and cutting-edge servo electronics, B&O complemented its Modernist aesthetics with mechanical proficiency. This profound transition was exemplified in its seminal Beogram 4000 turntable, which merited reintroduction by the company in 2020.

In Switzerland, Willi Studer's brand Revox became synonymous with professional and recording-studio quality for domestic application. As the Studer and Revox names became premier representatives of tape technology and reel-to-reel machines in particular, the company expanded its product line in the 1970s with an advanced direct-drive and linear-tracking turntable: the B790. Keeping to the theme of smaller but professional-grade tables of the 1970s, the studio-grade Revox maintained a modest market footprint, avoiding the mass-loaded and substantial broadcast tables of the 1960s.

○○ Tonearm Evolution

A tonearm is deceptively simple and can easily be dismissed as a stick holding a far more complex cartridge with an intricate stylus traversing a record until it reaches the central label. But by the 1970s, cartridges evolved to become "high-compliance," meaning that their styli became very flexible and required lighter arms to enable them to track properly. The heavy tonearms of previous decades would effectively crush these new styli into the grooves. As a result of the industry's shift toward high-compliance cartridges, tonearms in the 1970s followed suit with lower-mass designs, addressing tracking accuracy and stability with fresh ideas. A variety of tonearm types and methods hit the market with pivoted S-shaped arms rising in popularity, straight types, and linear-tracking arms.

Fundamental to any tonearm type is the requirement for it to maintain constant and consistent downward force at all times. This balance is usually achieved by an adjustable counterweight, which lends stability to the tracking force, allowing the center of gravity to remain in the groove. Supplementing an arm's need to remain centered, with appropriate downforce, was the introduction of an additional adjustment feature: an anti-skating mechanism. As a stylus tracks into a record, frictional drag is inevitable, tending to deviate and lean toward the inner groove, creating an imbalance. Anti-skating devices maintained equal stylus pressure against both sides of a groove. With the introduction of anti-skating arms in the 1970s, increased adjustability permitted fine-tuning for the high-compliance cartridges of the day.

In addition, it is incumbent upon a tonearm to move across a record in a straight line and maintain proper cartridge alignment in tangent to the grooves. But tracking in a straight line poses a dilemma as tonearms swivel on a pivot, resulting in a curved trajectory toward the last groove. As the cartridge angle deviates from true tangency, tracking errors occur, resulting in distortion and poor fidelity. In the 1970s this particular issue was given a great deal of attention, resulting in the research and development of linear-tracking tonearms. To frame the concept somewhat artlessly, linear arms attempt to reduce tracking error by moving the styli in a straight radial line across the record's surface in a manner not dissimilar to how a record is pressed initially, rejecting the arc trajectory of pivoted arms in favor of a consistent orientation.

Although the companies Ortho-Sonic and Burne Jones explored methods to address such tracking errors in the 1950s, linear-tracking arms would appear on the market more convincingly in the 1970s (one exception was the 1963 Marantz SLT-12). Leading off this renewal was the arm produced by Rabco, which was perhaps the most successful, especially if judged by its later influence on servo-driven linear-tracking designs such as the Goldmund T3 and T5 and the Pierre Lurné arms of the 1980s and 1990s. Harman Kardon obviously saw merit in linear-tracking arms, as it purchased Rabco and released the ST-5, ST-6, ST-7, and ST-8, all with linear arms. Garrard introduced the Zero model with its own take on this method. Lenco's efforts resulted in the lesser-known Sweeper, but its Swiss rival Revox launched the far more successful B790, B791, and B795, all with tangential arms. B&O proved to be a strong advocate as well, building upon the 1963 tangential arm by Acoustical and ultimately materializing in the 1974 Beogram 4000.

○○   Transition to Solid-State and Multitrack

Two decades earlier, in the 1950s, radio stations had already replaced their vacuum-tube-based equipment with transistorized solid-state machines. But the transition to transistors for recording apparatuses took a more lethargic pace, with solid-state devices eventually emerging in the recording studio by the early 1970s. This conversion was mostly due to the momentum of multitrack recordings, with sixteen and twenty-four tracks steadily becoming standard. The transition was swift: only a few years earlier, in 1968, the Beatles adventured into eight tracks with the song "While My Guitar Gently Weeps."[85] That recording essentially gave license to the industry, with no ceiling for allowable numbers of tracks in sight.

Inherent in multiple-track recordings was the ability to expand the creative possibilities, allowing endless experimentation, layering, and correction. But this realignment of recording priorities was followed by a loss of fidelity and a deviation from the purist high-fidelity movement that had been building since the 1950s. Greg Milner said, "Solid-state is really where recorded music meets the devil at the crossroads, getting the gift of convenience and flexibility in exchange for… it's not exactly clear, but in their darker moments, some engineers would say 'soul.'" [86]

Along with the turn to solid-state convenience came another reason for the poorer sound of multitrack recordings: the compression of each track resulting from a tape limited to 2 inches (5.1 cm) wide. The loss of bandwidth was especially evident when the track number increased from sixteen to twenty-four. While the sonic fidelity of LPs fell victim, LP sales were unaffected, which signaled to the industry a decisive turning point toward convenience and mass distribution of music. The inverse world, of increasing sophistication and variety in turntable and tonearm design, was somewhat oblivious to the market reality, which demonstrated for the first time its disconnection from what was happening in the recording studio.

This conspiracy of elements would have lasting effects, resulting in analog culture's descent and ultimate capitulation to the looming form of the compact disc (CD). With their digital panacea, the CD, Philips and Sony were eager to turn the page on the analog era. Supported by marketing promises of better sound and convenience, consumers readily embraced the next medium for recorded music, bidding farewell to a hundred years of analog cultivation and aestheticism.

Akai

Founded by Masukichi Akai in 1929, as a manufacturer of radio components and electronics, the Akai Electric Company transitioned to building phonograph motors by the late 1940s.[87] Establishing prominence in tape technology, primarily with its reel-to-reel decks, Akai transferred some of its skills to turntable design as well. In the 1970s it brought to the market both direct-drive and belt-drive models, with the direct-drive and fully automatic AP-307 demonstrating Akai's forward-design savvy and technological skills.

3.1	AP-307 TURNTABLE, AKAI, c.1978
3.2	AP-004X TURNTABLE, AKAI, 1973

3.1

3.2

○○ Bang & Olufsen (B&O)

Singular as an audio manufacturer in the sense of balancing technology with Modernist form, B&O can be credited with creating a class of consumer audio products that never strayed from distinctive Danish design. In the 1970s the name Beogram was given to its new line of turntables. Distancing itself from its dependency on the Thorens TD 124—which it had basically parroted in its 1960s models—B&O showed an entirely unique vision with its Beogram 4000, designed by Jacob Jensen and released in 1972. The 4000 incorporated an electronic tangential arm, becoming the tonearm of choice for future Beogram models, accompanied by a detector arm. Sticking to the same formula for two more decades, B&O's later Beogram 6000 and 7000 models shared the same design DNA as the 4000. As seminal examples of analog design, both the 1972 Beogram 4000 and the 1974 Beogram 6000 are in the collection of the Museum of Modern Art in New York.[88] Owing to its legacy and the recent analog revival, B&O rereleased the Beogram 4000 series turntable as a re-created limited edition in 2020.

3.3

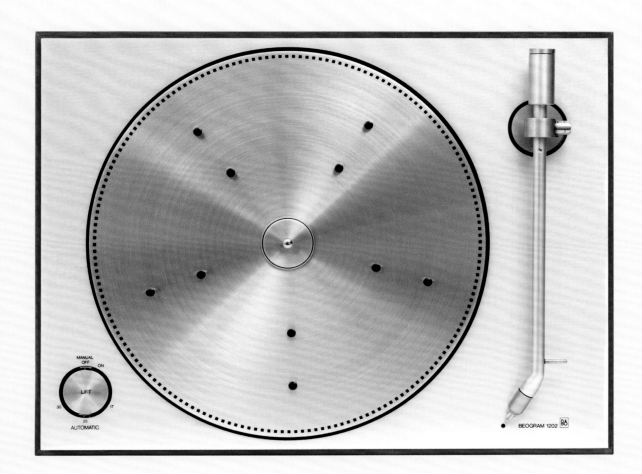

3.4

3.5

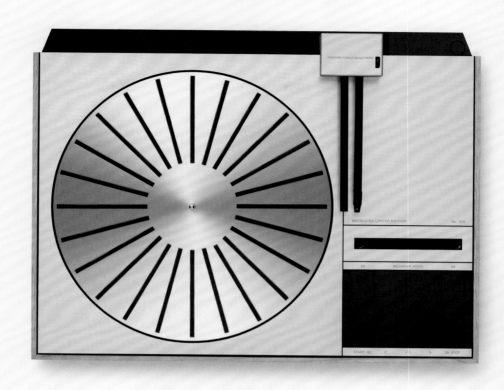

3.6

3.7

○○ Denon

Viewed through the lens of historical primacy, Denon is Japan's eminent pioneer. Much of Japan's rich analog culture stems from Denon's early contributions, namely the first Japanese phonograph in 1910. Denon also made the first audio recording of the emperor Hirohito at the end of World War II.[89] With its close connection to Nippon Columbia, Denon initially applied resources to broadcasting and professional sectors. But it shifted toward the consumer market with the 1970 launch of the DL-103 moving-coil cartridge. The DL-103 has been in production for more than fifty-six years, taking on a legendary status among vinyl collectors.[90] Denon's foray into broadcast-quality tables, such as the DN-302F, created the blueprint for its 1970s commercial turntables, such as the DP-5000 and the DP-3000. Sharing a solitary AC-motor direct-drive mechanism, these tables allowed for immediate and correct rpm as soon as the speed button was activated.[91] Denon later introduced tonearms and lavishly stained wooden plinths, which set its turntable designs apart from most of the mass-market Japanese tables of the 1970s.

3.8   DP-3000 DRIVE UNIT AND DA-309 TONEARM, DENON, 1972 (WITH CUSTOM PLINTH BY CLASSIC SOUND)

3.8

○○   Dual

With Dual's extraordinary emphasis on idler-drive mechanisms in the 1960s and the fame it cemented with the 1000 series—along with its most conspicuous example, the 1019—the company surprisingly took a turn toward direct drive by the 1970s. The 704 and CS 731Q models demonstrate this change, with a quartz phase lock loop incorporated into the latter, hinting at the growing influence of Japanese direct-drive imports and Dual's ultimate capitulation to this type of drive.

3.9	CS 704 TURNTABLE, DUAL, 1976
3.10	CS 721 TURNTABLE, DUAL, 1976

3.9

3.10

○○ Dunlop

When it comes to Scotland's contribution to turntable design, Linn gets the lion's share of attention. But another Scottish entity, founded by Peter Dunlop, entered the market with somewhat less flair but clearly not lacking in innovation or analog capability. Dunlop's Systemdek turntable featured a belt-drive mechanism, three-point spring suspension, unique three-layer isolated plinth with dampers, Airpax 24-pole motor, and a ⅜-inch (10-millimeter) spindle with ball bearing and oil pump. Introduced in 1979, the Systemdek eventually underwent various changes and iterations but maintained its cylinder form, a feature that would be imitated by future turntable brands.

3.11   SYSTEMDEK II TURNTABLE, DUNLOP, c.1983 (THIS MODEL, 1985)

3.11

○○   Goldring

Originally established in Berlin in 1906, Goldring found its way to the United Kingdom and became an early manufacturer of magnetic cartridges. By the 1950s its cartridges became well-known, especially its early MC versions. Its most popular foray into turntables was a collaboration with Lenco on the L75, or the Goldring-branded GL75. The GL75 featured an infinitely adjustable speed mechanism by way of a conical spindle, dynamically balanced tonearm, and knife-edge bearings. Despite the table's popularity and acclaim, Goldring later turned its attention exclusively to cartridge design.

3.12   GL75 TURNTABLE, GOLDRING WITH LENCO, 1967

3.12

○○   Electrohome

During the early 1970s, a plethora of brands were captivated with space-age and sci-fi futurism. Incorporating these themes into its Apollo range of players was Electrohome, an established Canadian consumer-electronics brand founded in 1907. With its smoked-acrylic orb-shaped dome and matching speakers, the Apollo became one of the more visible brands representing 1970s space-age adventurism.

3.13

3.14

○○   Europhon

Founded in Milan in 1949, the highly stylized consumer-electronics manufacturer introduced Italian flair into its radios, televisions, and turntables. A parallel may be drawn with another Italian firm, Olivetti, which brought a similar edge in voguish industrial design to its typewriters. Not shy about effulgent colors, Europhon models often indulged in plastic housing and smart dials. Its 1970s Autunno turntable, with an integrated speaker, exemplified the appeal that Europhon had for many design-oriented consumers.

3.15–16   AUTUNNO TURNTABLE, EUROPHON, 1970s [BELOW AND OPPOSITE]

3.15

EUROPHON

○○   Japan Victor Company (JVC)

Similar to Denon and Nippon, JVC maintained high standing in the hierarchy of dominant Japanese audio entities. Founded in 1927, JVC achieved fame in various domains, most notably with the VHS format of consumer video recorders in the 1970s, with its presence in the professional-recording arena, and with its 1971 discrete system for four-channel quadraphonic sound on vinyl. While JVC was perhaps not as recognized for its hi-fi products, its contribution to 1970s turntable design is quite remarkable. In 1974 JVC introduced the world's first quartz-lock turntable, which avoided errors that often resulted from the many variables associated with correcting the platter speed. The company's QL and JL series of 1970s tables offered both direct-drive and belt-drive systems, combined with its gimbal-supported tonearm that allowed for flexible adjustments. JVC's revolutionary quartz-lock technology found its way into countless Japanese turntables, affirming its considerable influence on analog culture.

3.17

3.18

3.19

○○ Kenwood

Another Japanese hi-fi manufacturer to emerge in the 1970s was Kenwood. Established in 1946 with an emphasis on radio equipment, it later became a producer of a wide range of popular hi-fi equipment. The company's peak in turntable designs was its 1970s KD series: the most significant example was the KD-500, otherwise known as "the Rock" for its polymer-cement-resin plinth. Kenwood's emphasis on an inert and resonance-free plinth influenced Sharp's 1975 Optonica model, as well as later stone designs such as J. C. Verdier's La Platine, Jadis's Thalie, and various Well Tempered Lab models.

| 3.20 | KD-5077 TURNTABLE, KENWOOD, c.1979 |
| 3.21–22 | KD-500 TURNTABLE, KENWOOD, 1976 |

3.20

3.21

3.22

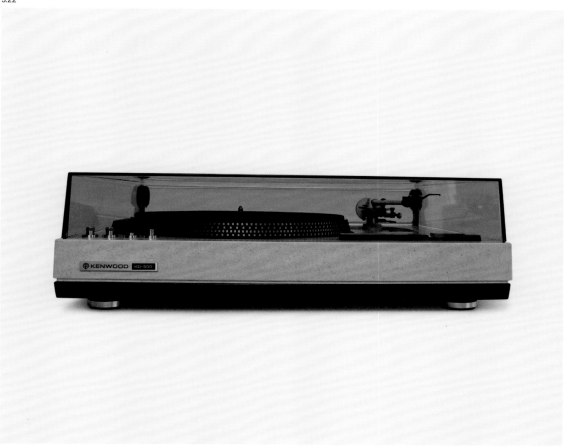

○○   Linn

　　　As discussed earlier, Ivor Tiefenbrun's Linn Sondek LP12 introduced the concept of high-end to turntable design.[92] Considered to be one of the most influential and significant turntables of all time, the LP12 evolved since its introduction in 1972 while maintaining many of the original design features, such as a suspended sub-chassis, single-point precision bearing, and belt-drive mechanism. In the 1970s the LP12 was frequently partnered with the Grace 707, Sumiko, or Mission tonearms, but Linn eventually introduced its own tonearm, the Ittok LVII, in 1979, which was followed by the Ekos and Akito arms. The company Naim created the unipivot Aro tonearm, which became quite popular on the LP12. In whatever guise the LP12 was outfitted, including numerous power-supply upgrades (such as Valhalla and Lingo) and tweaks throughout the decades, "it's impossible to imagine the high-end industry without the LP12."[93]

3.23　　　SONDEK LP12 TURNTABLE, LINN, 1973

3.23

○○   Rabco

Carrying the linear-tracking torch passed on by Ortho-Sonic and Burne Jones, Rabco was the most prominent 1970s entity to champion tangential tracking. The premise behind this method of tracking is to duplicate as closely as possible how the record was initially cut. When a record is cut, the cutter diamond maintains a ninety-degree angle from start to finish. A tangential playback tonearm attempts to track these grooves in the same ninety-degree manner, thereby reducing tracking error. Rabco's SL-8 and SL-8E tonearms represented the period's most popular linear tracking arms as they incorporated servo motors controlling lateral movement and cuing mechanisms. Seeing Rabco's rising popularity, Harman Kardon purchased the company in the early 1970s and released the ST-7 turntable. The most striking parallel with the Rabco tonearm would occur a decade later with the belt-driven T3 and T5 servo arms designed by Goldmund and Pierre Lurné.

| 3.24 | ST-7 TURNTABLE, HARMAN/KARDON RABCO, 1976 |
| 3.25 | ST-4 TURNTABLE, RABCO, c.1970s |

3.24

3.25

○○ Pioneer

The Pioneer corporation was once at the forefront of Japan's hi-fi and video export machine. Along with other key Japanese brands that have faded in the new millennium, Pioneer showed its true mettle in 1970s turntable design, eventually watering down its products to more mainstream models by the 1980s. Its PL series of turntables stayed true to the Japanese direct-drive tradition, with some models enhanced with quartz-lock technology. Its accompanying tonearms incorporated many of the sophisticated features surfacing in the 1970s, such as lateral balancing, anti-skating mechanisms, stylus-pressure indicators, and oil-damped cuing. Impressive wooden plinths provided Pioneer tables with inert foundations, further bestowing the brand with a reputation for excellence.

3.26

3.27

3.28

○○ Philips

When Philips released its rainbow assortment of fashion-oriented turntables in the 1950s, it was clear that the company was going after a younger demographic. Continuing the same theme into the 1960s and 1970s, Philips expanded its offerings with a kaleidoscopic range of colors (as demonstrated by the 815, which sported a host of tone controls) along with battery-powered portability, most famously identified by the multi-speed 113 model. By the 1980s Philips's quaint palette would disappear in favor of more staid and somber aluminum finishes.

3.29

3.30

3.31

○○   Revox

Few hi-fi companies can match the engineering pedigree of Switzerland's storied Revox. In the realm of tape technology, recording, and open-reel machines, Revox and its professional branch, Studer, excelled by providing products for recording studios in addition to domestic hi-fi equipment. In purchasing a Revox product, consumers implicitly understood that they were purchasing audio devices not far removed from the professional realm, which offered an air of legitimacy and validation. At the helm of Revox sat Willi Studer, the company's founder and visionary leader. Perhaps because of its professional affiliation, Revox designed a linear-tracking-based turntable; by the 1970s the company was ready to introduce the B790, followed by the B795. These complex models featured a quartz-controlled direct-drive mechanism with a servo-controlled linear-tracking tonearm. Revox commissioned the headphone specialist AKG to supply the table with a moving-magnet cartridge, the MDR20. The B series of 1970s Revox turntables are prime examples of austere yet highly functional Swiss designs.

3.32	B790 TURNTABLE, REVOX, 1977
3.33–34	B795 TURNTABLE, REVOX, 1979

3.32

3.33

3.34

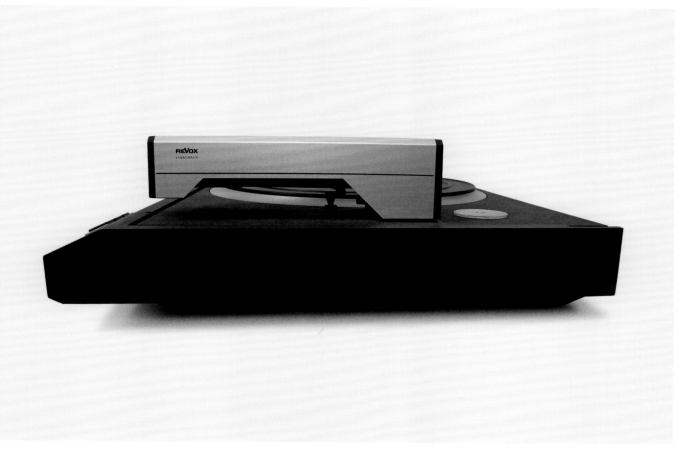

○○ Sharp

More often associated with calculators and printers from the 1980s, the Sharp brand infrequently rolls off the tongue in analog parlors. But its 1970s Optonica RP-3500 and RP-3636 rightfully deserve mention, despite being the company's few legitimate attempts at a high-end turntable design. In contrast to other Japanese brands that outsourced their production, Sharp designed and built these models in-house. Weighing 35 pounds (15.9 kilograms) due to its composite and stonelike granite plinth and equipped with a magnesium S-shaped tonearm, these direct-drive models were a formidable contribution to the era's Japanese designs and are fancied by collectors today.[94]

3.35 — OPTONICA RP-3500 TURNTABLE, SHARP, c.1975

3.35

○○   Thorens

By the 1970s Thorens's idler-driven TD 124 and TD 124 MKII tables were ready to retire. The broadcast persona was to be abandoned in favor of suspended designs, now championed by Acoustic Research and Linn. In 1972 Thorens released the TD 160, which would enjoy a production run of nearly twenty years. It employed a belt-drive mechanism and a floating sub-chassis with three adjustable springs. Coupled to a sprung chassis, the tonearm and platter were isolated and independent of the plinth. In 1972 Thorens updated its belt-driven and three-point-suspended TD 125 model, primarily with the new four-point gimbal-bearing TP16 tonearm and a retailored oscillator-motor-controlled circuitry for greater speed stability. Other new models appeared in the 1970s, including the TD 104, TD 105, TD 110, TD 115, TD 126, TD 145, TD 165, and TD 166, along with tonearms such as the TP62 Isotrack. Some of these models gained a contemporary following as tenacious as that of the TD 124.

3.36	TD 125 MKI TURNTABLE, THORENS (WITH 3009 TONEARM, SME), EARLY 1970s (RESTORED AND UPGRADED BY BERLIN VINTAGE TURNTABLES, c.2021)
3.37	TD 125 MKII TURNTABLE, THORENS, RESTORED AND UPGRADED BY ARTISAN FIDELITY, 2013

3.36

3.37

○○   Ortofon

This legendary Danish firm continued to evolve from its SPU analog designs established in the 1950s. By the 1970s Ortofon introduced the AS-212 S-shaped tonearm with an innovative adjustable magnetic anti-skating device. Accommodating cartridges of five to twelve grams, it was well suited for modern moving-coil (MC) types prevailing in the 1970s. But it was the company's MC 20 that firmly entrenched Ortofon as a premier cartridge manufacturer. Designed by Hisayoshi Nakatsuka, the MC 20 was a low-output type requiring a step-up transformer, which the company supplied as well. (Nakatsuka would re-emerge in the 2000s analog revival with his own cartridge brand, ZYX.) A decade later, Ortofon would again transform its offerings, often appearing with a Technics direct-drive table in the DJ-inspired club scene of the 1980s.

| 3.38 | MC 20 MKII CARTRIDGE, ORTOFON, 1976 |
| 3.39 | CONCORDE MC 200 CARTRIDGE, ORTOFON, 1979 |

3.38

3.39

○○   Supex

Japanese cartridge history contains an artisanal legacy that remains unchallenged in the West. That is not to say that the varied cartridges by Grado, Shure, Ortofon, or even Jan Allaerts are not imbued with their own storied traditions. But when it comes to the story of Yoshiaki Sugano, the driving force behind Supex's key cartridges and his later Koetsu designs, the artisanal DNA becomes, in a sense, a birthright. His 1970s SD-900 and SD-909 MC cartridges emphasized metals of the highest purity, especially copper for the coils of the generators. Rubber dampers for the coils were intentionally aged in order to ensure long-term stability. Sugano additionally employed a specially crafted magnet of cerium cobalt and a finely polished elliptical stylus. Supex was so highly regarded that even Linn outsourced its cartridge designs to the company. By the 1980s Sugano moved on from Supex and created the brand Koetsu.

| 3.40 | SD-909 MC CARTRIDGE, YOSHIAKI SUGANO, SUPEX, c.1970s |
| 3.41 | SD-900 MC CARTRIDGE, YOSHIAKI SUGANO, SUPEX, c.1970s |

3.40

3.41

1980s and 1990s

○○ Beauty in the Breakdown

It would be easy to simply dismiss these two decades, painfully characterizing them as the historical period of analog extinction. The discussion would regurgitate hackneyed statistics about the ascent of the compact disc (CD) and its eventual vanquishment of vinyl, while readers are likely familiar with Philips's and Sony's implied yet illusory promise of "perfect sound forever." The superiority of CDs, as promoted by the companies' marketing teams, was gradually absorbed by consumers who were eager to accept the assurances. But surprisingly this period led to a positive outcome for analog culture, one not protected in layers of denial to feign validity.

What the CD's nearly hegemonic domination of this period meant for turntable and analog culture was a natural decline in both analog recording techniques and analog playback. But the loss of analog technique and the questionable fidelity of its digital successor was met with considerable resistance. On point, Brian Eno said, "I hate the way CDs just drone on for bloody hours and you stop caring." [95] With this many would conclude that turntable development faded away, following a story not dissimilar to that of horse-driven buggies being replaced by automobiles in the early part of the twentieth century. Paradoxically, turntables not only survived but also reached a high point of development and evolution. By the 1980s there had been a century of phonograph progress, which would not just suddenly come to a halt. The momentum in turntable, tonearm, and cartridge design had peaked with unprecedented maturity by the late 1970s. That high-end innovating was now ripe, a decade later, for even more extreme application and design. A cottage turntable industry emerged, setting itself apart from mainstream domestic products and inexpensive Asian imports.

Established electronics giants from Japan such as Marantz, Luxman, Nakamichi, Sony, and Technics excelled in introducing critical representations of their analog talents, with Micro Seiki leading in the consummate Japanese approach. The American firm VPI, with its New Jersey factory in proximity to Thomas Edison's original plant, put the United States back on the analog map. Switzerland's Goldmund picked up where Thorens and Revox left off, with its Studio turntable, Reference turntable, and Rabco-inspired T3 tangential tonearm. The French-made La Platine Verdier enthusiastically redefined 1970s Japanese stone plinths, and the British old guard was now challenged by newcomers such as Maplenoll, MRM (with its Source turntable), Pink Triangle, and Roksan. The Swedish company Forsell entered the extreme-design melee with its Air Reference Tangential Air Bearing turntable, and tonearms attained NASA-level engineering, with designs from Eminent Technology, Rockport Technologies, and Fidelity Research distancing themselves from tonearms of the preceding, experimental decades.

In regard to standard Japanese imports, it would be unfair to label all of them as exemplars of mainstream mediocrity. While most were flimsy devices sold en masse, a select group were well designed and fun to operate. In this realm, turntables by Aiwa, Akai, Kenwood, Sansui, and Sony boasted pure spaceship-console art with colored lights, soft-touch push buttons, and fully automatic functionality.

○○ Cartridge Design

By the 1950s piezoelectric crystal and ceramic cartridges had been replaced by two magnetic types, moving magnet (MM) or moving coil (MC). Either type of cartridge sports high compliance, and 1970s tonearm designs accommodated their lightness and nuanced tracking ability. In the 1980s MM types became pigeonholed into the low- to mid-fidelity audio classifications, whereas MC types found favor in high-end salons. Both MM and

MC cartridges consist of a housing, stylus, cantilever, suspension, magnet, and coils. The stylus serves a delicate and critical role in tracking a record's groove modulations. The vibrations it encounters travel through the cantilever upon which the stylus is attached, continuing their journey to the magnet or coil assembly. These delicate and very-low-level signals are then sent to a pre-amplifier, which produces the audible sound.

Compared to high-impedance MM cartridges, MC types have comparatively low inductance and impedance. High impedance can negatively influence linearity of phase response and frequency response. While MC cartridges generally and favorably have lower moving masses, their lower signal output requires higher preamplifier gain, often at the expense of added noise. Which cartridge type offers superior fidelity is an age-old audiophile polemic, one that is purely subjective and better left to the user to decide.

More certain was the number of MC cartridge brands appearing in the 1980s and 1990s. The Japanese held quite the monopoly in the artisanal realm, with brands such as Audio Technica, Denon, Dynavector, Kiseki, Koetsu, and Miyabi. Ortofon continued to expand its offerings, along with the industry's standards such as Goldring, Grado, and Shure. But a new generation of cartridge makers emerged in Europe, including Benz Micro, Clearaudio, Van den Hul, and Jan Allaerts. Many would continue into the new millennium, with countless more brands emerging during analog's revival.

○○   Technics SL-1200 and Analog Culture

Despite vinyl relinquishing its dominance to the CD among consumers, DJ culture shunned the new medium of ones and zeros and formed a holy relationship with vinyl. Disc jockeys preferred the 1970s Technics SL-1200 turntable, for it allowed them to mix records with complete speed control: the direct-drive table could instantly return to a set speed after a record was moved back and forth on the platter (the technique known as scratching).[96] The table's quartz-controlled high-torque motor enabled ideal manipulation through scratching and beat mixing, and the solid plinth made it impervious to club resonances and vibrations. With the hip-hop, dance, and techno scenes embracing the SL-1200, the table became a part of the social fabric, in essence preserving vinyl within youth culture and allowing it to sustain the onslaught of digital audio. In an effort to determine the origin of the DJs' love affair for this table, historians like to point to Grandmaster Flash's record, "The Adventures of Grandmaster Flash on the Wheels of Steel."[97] This single from the grandfather of hip-hop was created, using a Technics SL-1200, from a medley of scratches and LP cuts, all intertwined from two records and coming together not just to create a song but also to give birth to a movement that now dominates popular musical culture.

One may speculate whether the SL-1200's designer, Shuichi Obata, and his team earmarked the turntable for professional or consumer application. But it is doubtful Obata foresaw the table's place a decade later at clubs such as New York City's the Tunnel, scratching records by Run-D.M.C. and fading into or playing over strains of Depeche Mode and New Order. Even if Obata did not see this use of the SL-1200 coming, he was certainly made aware of it by the time the MK2 version was on the drawing board. In revising the SL-1200 in the late 1970s, Obata met with DJs in order to sensitize the table to their requirements. As a result, the SL-1200MK2 was reengineered with the club scene as its inspiration. Apropos to its DJ purpose, Technics claimed it to be "tough enough to take a disco beat and accurate enough to keep it."[98] Obata's legendary SL-1200 continues to evolve, serving as one of the stronger and most visible catalysts for analog's revival and renaissance in the 2000s.

○○ The Source, by MRM Audio

Perhaps one of the shortest production runs of the 1980s was the Source turntable by MRM Audio. Designed by Mike Moore in 1983, the British model appeared to be influenced by Hamish Robertson's Ariston RD11 and Strathclyde Transcription Developments' STD 305M but differed by using an extremely robust alloy sub-chassis and heavy alloy platter. As a result of the heavier platter—and to accommodate better weight distribution with less rocking—Moore opted for four springs (as in the STD 305M), differing from the Ariston's lighter platter that featured a three-spring design. The table was belt-driven by a Papst DC motor and utilized a power supply consisting of parallel high-quality EI transformers.[99] In 1986 Moore sold the company, and his turntable eventually receded into relative obscurity. Although his mark on the analog world was ephemeral, it was this type of individualistic passion that allowed creativity, from both large and small players, to flourish in the 1980s.

4.1   THE SOURCE TURNTABLE, MIKE MOORE, THE SOURCE, BY MRM AUDIO, 1983

4.1

Forsell

This Swedish-made turntable and tonearm were the products of Dr. Peter Forsell. As a surgeon, Forsell was sensitized to precision tooling and desired to bring this level of machining to turntable and tonearm design. He incorporated an air-bearing platter and air-bearing linear-tracking tonearm in his Air Reference turntable. During the 1990s the Forsell was considered one of the top high-end turntables available.

4.2–3   AIR REFERENCE TURNTABLE, FORSELL, c.1994

4.2

4.3

○○ Aiwa

Perhaps better known for introducing the first Japanese cassette recorder in 1964, along with its consumer electronics products, Aiwa achieved widespread popularity in the 1980s with its portable players and hi-fi components. Of special note were its turntables, with the LP-3000 best representing Aiwa's most ambitious efforts. The quartz phase-lock-loop (PLL) and direct-drive table hosted a unique linear static tonearm, which was similar to Sony's tangential Biotracer on its PS-X800 table. Only a handful of Japanese entities dared to venture into tangential tonearm production, and Aiwa would be one of the more conspicuous examples.

4.4	AP-2200 TURNTABLE, AIWA, 1977
4.5	LP-3000E TURNTABLE, AIWA, 1979
4.6	AP-D60 TURNTABLE, AIWA, c.1981

4.4

4.5

4.6

○○   Sota

When Sota first came on the scene in the early 1980s, it was the only high-end turntable manufactured in the United States. Its first turntable was the Sapphire, which is still in production today, in its MKIV iteration. Built of solid wood, the original Sapphire was an impressively inert design. Utilizing a belt-drive design with Papst motor, it was quite similar to other tables of the period. Implementing a sprung suspension that hung from its mass-loaded design, and deviating somewhat from a classic sprung design, it had an affinity to the similarly spring-loaded Oracle Delphi. Testament to the table's solidity was its imperviousness to external vibrations and resonances; the table was known to absorb taps on its solid-wood body without any audible effects. Available as an option was a vacuum pump, which evacuated all air between the platter and the record and reduced the effects of warped and uneven records. Today Sota is still revered as one of the oldest and most respected high-end turntable manufacturers in the United States.

4.7   SAPPHIRE TURNTABLE, SOTA, 1980s

4.7

○○   Audiomeca / Pierre Lurné

Having built his first tonearm at age twenty in 1968, Pierre Lurné never had any doubts about his passion. By 1979 he formed his company Audiomeca and became a go-to resource for Goldmund's überanalog designs, most famously with the T3 tangential tonearm. By the late 1980s Lurné eventually released his own dedicated models, such as the J1 turntable and the SL5 (Goldmund T5 variant) linear-tracking tonearm. Using a generous application of methacrylate in the construction along with lead in the platter of the J1, Lurné put great emphasis on vibration control.[100] The J1 also implemented a creative idler-pulley system that supplemented the primary motor-driven belt, deviating and distancing the J1 from the earlier direct-drive Goldmund Studio table.

| 4.8 | ROMA TURNTABLE, PIERRE LURNÉ, AUDIOMECA, 1990s |

4.8

4.9

4.10

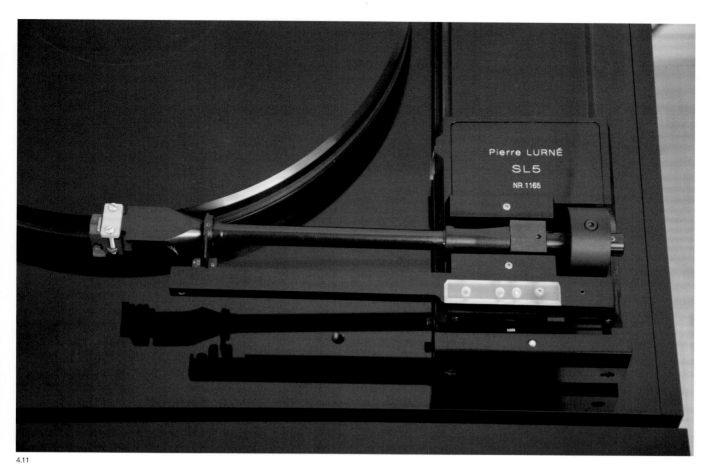

4.11

4.12

○○ Goldmund

Founded in 1978 with the vision of Michel Reverchon, the Swiss company can be credited, along with a few others, for creating a class and distinct tier of extreme audio products. The products that elevated Goldmund into that echelon were the Studio turntable, T3 tangential tonearm, Reference turntable, and Studietto turntable with T5 tangential tonearm. Reverchon's skill was in sourcing talent to design Goldmund's products, enlisting engineering heavyweights such as Georges Bernard and Pierre Lurné. The T3 was, in essence, a modern derivative of the Rabco design, a servo-controlled linear-tracking parallel tonearm, which used sensors to guide its lateral movement. The Studio turntable featured a direct-drive system powered by a Papst motor (later replaced by a JVC motor). Lurné's contribution was evident in terms of the methacrylate and lead-ingot platter, along with the three-point spring-loaded suspension. Goldmund's concept of "mechanical grounding" was first implemented in its turntables; this meant providing an evacuation route for vibrations, resonances, and other mechanical energy trapped in the device, which would otherwise find their way back into the cartridge and resultant playback. Elected as one of the components that "shook the world," the Reference turntable was unprecedented in the analog market.[101] Limited to three hundred examples, the colossal table was finished in gold, brass, and black anodized aluminum. Its belt-drive motor was encased in a mechanically suspended housing, spinning a 33-pound (15-kilogram) platter constructed from methacrylate and brass. The company's latest T3F tonearm was mounted on a 1⅝-inch (40-millimeter) support, and all functions were placed on a gold and smoked-glass panel. The 66-pound (30-kilogram) aluminum sub-chassis implemented Goldmund's application of mechanical grounding, using a rear-central spike to release the table's stored energy. Widely considered Georges Bernard's masterpiece of audio engineering, the Reference stands as one of the most extreme realizations of analog design.

4.13	STUDIETTO TURNTABLE AND T5 TONEARM, GOLDMUND, 1988
4.14	REFERENCE TURNTABLE AND T3 TONEARM, GOLDMUND, 1982 [OPPOSITE]

4.13

○○ Luxman

Like other prominent Japanese brands, such as Accuphase and Nakamichi, Luxman rose to fame in the 1970s and 1980s primarily due to the brand's excellent tube and solid-state offerings. Considered a high-end entity since its founding in 1925, Luxman separated itself from the pack through its craftsmanship and aesthetics, and its turntables followed suit. Similar to many other Japanese tables, Luxman preferred the system of direct-drive (though the brand offered some belt-drive models), but it differed dramatically with its Vacuum Disc Stabilizer (VDS). This mechanism of coupling a record to the platter—by removing the air between the record and the platter—attempted to alleviate the issues arising from warped records. The PD-300 and the PD-555 were the brand's most visible applications of its VDS technology and its favored classic models. Luxman's elegant industrial design, which combined metal plinths with wood bases and fascia, found favor with discerning audiophiles worldwide and continues to remain peerless in its form factor and design.

| 4.15 | PD444 TURNTABLE, LUXMAN, 1977 |
| 4.16–17 | PD-555 TURNTABLE, LUXMAN, 1980 |

4.15

4.16

4.17

4.18

4.19

4.20

○○ Nakamichi

When one thinks of Nakamichi, what first comes to mind is its range of classic tape decks: the famous 1000ZXL, Dragon, or mechanically impressive RX series with rotating cassettes. These tape decks helped define the audio scene in the 1970s and 1980s. Not as well-known were its two statement turntables released in the 1980s, the reference TX-1000 and the more affordable Dragon CT. Like its reference tape decks, these turntables were all-out in design, without compromise. The TX-1000 was the vision of Etsuro Nakamichi, the company's founder, but was built by Micro Seiki. The design and manufacturing of the Dragon CT were outsourced to Junichi Okumura and Fujiya Audio. A feature shared by both tables is a mechanism that measures a record's "groove eccentricity" to reposition an LP due to off-center or worn spindle holes, which may cause pitch distortions. This feature was activated by a sensor arm, which was deployed over the record and measured the spindle hole for off-centeredness. Once this was determined, the platter would automatically be moved into a centered position. The TX-1000 used one platter whereas the Dragon CT used two, with the direct-drive, quartz phase-lock-loop (PLL) motor of the TX-1000 housed in an oil bath within a Pressure Regulation Chamber. Similar to Micro Seiki designs, the TX-1000 was constructed with a monolithic die-cast aluminum base, unlike the Dragon CT with its wooden base. An optional vacuum record stabilizer (VS-100) rounded out the TX-1000's comprehensive features. These two turntables equaled the engineering and design excellence found in Nakamichi's tape decks and found their way into the segment of highest-ranking Japanese turntables, dominated by brands such as Micro Seiki and Technics.

4.21

4.22

○○ Micro Seiki

Founded in 1961, Micro Seiki rose as a subcontractor for other turn-table manufacturers such as Luxman, Denon, Sharp, and Kenwood. In 1975 the brand was featured in *Playboy* magazine as an appropriate candidate for the world's most expensive hi-fi systems, and the brand rose in stature among analog cognoscenti.[102] Contemporaneously developing its own line of turntables, it aspired toward even higher-end designs by the 1980s and 1990s. *Audio* magazine claimed that the RX-5000 turntable was "trimmed for longevity in all mechanical properties so that it could outlast some of its owners—to the delight of its heirs."[103] Joining the company in 1980 was Hideaki Nishikawa, who oversaw the development of Micro Seiki's flagship product, the SX-8000 turntable. (Nishikawa later went on to form TechDAS, which is currently one of Japan's most illustrious turntable brands.) Released in 1984 the SX-8000 II was a 295-pound (133.8-kilogram) behemoth that incorporated an air-suction mechanism to secure records to the platter. Similar to that used in Luxman's designs, the Micro Seiki suction system featured better air circulation and more durable mechanics. The company applied the same principles to its 194-pound (88-kilogram) SZ-1 series of tables, which featured an air-isolated floating platter and massive motor assembly. The RX-1500 series proved very popular for the brand and utilized its quadruplex suspension system, including coil springs, rubber-diaphragm-supported piston, compressed air, and high-viscosity oil. The RX-1500 VG and RX-1500 FVG also took advantage of the company's famous vacuum pump along with an air-bearing design that allowed the heavy platter to float above the plinth, thereby virtually eliminating friction. Held in high esteem and universally prized for its turntables and tonearms, Micro Seiki occupies a venerated status in the annals of turntable design.

| 4.23 | RX-5000 TURNTABLE PLATTER UNIT, MICRO SEIKI, EARLY 1980s |
| 4.24 | RX-5000 TURNTABLE PLATTER UNIT AND RY-5500 MOTOR UNIT, MICRO SEIKI, EARLY 1980s [OPPOSITE] |

4.23

4.26

4.27

○○ Oracle

Widely considered Canada's most visible contribution to analog artistry, Oracle's Delphi model is representative of a long legacy of turntable craftsmanship and passion. Oracle was created in 1979 by Marcel Riendeau, a lecturer of philosophy at the University of Sherbrooke in Quebec. The Delphi MKI turntable was released in 1980 to great acclaim; the renowned audio reviewer J. Peter Moncrieff, after listening to its prototype, exclaimed that it was "634 times better than the Linn."[104] For this table, Oracle implemented a belt drive and a new take on a suspended sub-chassis, choosing to place the springs away from the platter and doing away with a table housing altogether. Rejecting the equidistant placement of springs from each other and the center spindle—the method espoused by Acoustic Research, Linn, and Thorens—Oracle broke the mold and quickly shared the limelight in the 1980s with other top-ranked turntables. Relying on a generous application of acrylic, combined with an aluminum platter and adjustable aluminum suspension towers, this turntable was one of the most visually compelling ever designed. Because the performance of the table was highly dependent upon the fine-tuning of the suspension and the technical savvy of its owners, Oracle continued to simplify its design through the decades. Currently in its MKVI iteration, the Delphi turntable continues to maintain its cachet among record collectors.

4.28	DELPHI MKII TURNTABLE, ORACLE, c.1984
4.29–30	DELPHI MK V TURNTABLE, ORACLE, c.1996

4.28

4.29

4.30

○○ Sony

If any company had the resources to build the world's best turntables, it was undoubtedly Sony, which was established after World War II and rose to become one of Japan's biggest exporters of consumer electronics. The multinational conglomerate and electronics powerhouse offered a multitude of consumer electronics during the 1980s and 1990s and was especially acclaimed for its famous Walkman. With that said, it would be easy to dismiss the company's turntables as afterthoughts. But to the contrary Sony's resources allowed it to build impressive tables during the 1970s and 1980s. Sony's brushless-slotless-linear (BSL) motors powered their direct-drive systems without torque cogging while being monitored by its proprietary Magnedisc servo-control mechanism, augmented in some models with quartz crystal in order to reduce wow and flutter. Furthermore, Sony achieved silent tonearm automation with its low-mass engineered designs and used the company's bulk-molding compound for its housing. This was a proprietary non-resonant material that addressed acoustic feedback in the turntable's structure. Fans of the brand often point to the PS-6750 as an example of Sony's more traditional styling in the 1970s and the early 1980s and the PS-FL7 as representative of Sony's modern analog aesthetic in the mid-1980s. Constructed from an aluminum alloy die-cast, the sleek PS-FL7 direct-drive table used an advanced linear-tracking arm, which featured fully automated and smooth operation. Though Sony eventually turned its attention away from its analog designs, the brand is still indicative of the period's turntable milieu.

| 4.31 | PS-FL7 TURNTABLE, SONY, 1985 |
| 4.32 | PS-F5 TURNTABLE, SONY, 1983 [OPPOSITE] |

4.31

4.33

4.34

4.35

○○ Pink Triangle

As expected, many well-established companies contributed significantly to the period's analog landscape. But new and compelling turntables emerged from smaller, more modest, and more colorful entities. Established in the United Kingdom in 1979 by Neal Jackson and Arthur Khoubesserian, the brand Pink Triangle was named for the symbol used by the Nazis to identify homosexuals.[105] The company's first turntable, the Pink Triangle "Original," innovatively employed Aerolam, an inert aluminum honeycomb material used in the construction of airplanes, for its sub-chassis. Perhaps Pink Triangle borrowed the concept from Celestion, a prominent British company that used Aerolam for its famous SL600 speakers. Achieving very rigid mass and low energy storage, the Pink Triangle "Original" featured other creative solutions, including hanging the sub-chassis by suspension springs, as opposed to the conventional method of resting it on compression springs. Pink Triangle later expanded its range to the PT1 and PT TOO tables. The final offering of the company was the Tarantella. Its acrylic structure was in the form of a triangle with red LED lights illuminating the acrylic chassis and platter. Gaining analog devotees worldwide, Pink Triangle contributed solid engineering in its products. But perhaps more importantly, the company lightened up an austere industry with its stylistic and chromatic approach.

4.36

4.37

○○   Mitsubishi
        Similar to Sony and Panasonic, Mitsubishi once represented one of
Japan's strongest consumer-electronics brands. With a history going back
to the 1800s, Mitsubishi's portfolio was quite extensive by the 1980s and
represented a broad range of electronic goods. Easy to dismiss as a mainstream afterthought, the company's turntables established a precedence of
vertically aligned form, which other Japanese firms emulated throughout the
1980s. Beginning with the all-in-one vertical X-10, the company later released
its most impressive vertical table, the LT-5V with a linear-tracking tonearm.

4.38   LT-5V TURNTABLE, MITSUBISHI, c.1980

4.38

◯◯   Technics

No other brand of turntable can convincingly compete for creating the mise-en-scène of analog culture from the 1970s to the 1990s. As discussed earlier in this chapter, Technics is the only brand that penetrated DJ culture so pervasively and cogently, becoming a cultural icon for hip-hop musicians and de rigueur for club consoles. Craig Kalman, the CEO of Atlantic Records, spoke passionately about his Technics: "As a DJ in New York City in the '80s, the Technics SL-1200 was my prized possession. Whether I was working the club scene at Danceteria, Palladium, or the Tunnel, the Technics never left my side. Growing up, I had two at home flanking my Urei mixer—[the Technics] was my staple, along with my vinyl. Years later, I'm still cuing records on a SL-1200, feeling the same boyish anticipation for the needle to drop."[106] As the representative of a movement, Shuichi Obata's SL-1200 endures to this day, with production now in its MK7 iteration. The intersection of turntable design and analog culture—so persuasive with the SL-1200 and popular musical and youth movements—created an undoubtable mark on history. It is one thing to discuss the glories of a turntable as an objet d'art in both design and collectible terms, but when an object of mechanical and industrial design mobilizes genres of music to develop and thrive, it takes on the role of cultural catalyst, enabling art to emerge.

| 4.39 | SL-1100 TURNTABLE, TECHNICS, 1971 |

4.39

4.40

4.41

4.42

4.43

○○ VPI Industries

By the early 1980s, New Jersey–based VPI Industries joined Sota as the only other US-based turntable manufacturer. Founded by Sheila and Harry Weisfeld in 1978, VPI began by making a record weight, a turntable isolation base (commissioned by Denon and JVC), and a record-cleaning machine. Its HW-16 cleaning machine picked up where the legendary Keith Monks device left off, becoming an indispensable machine for practically all vinyl enthusiasts. Eventually transitioning to turntable design, VPI released the HW-19, a two-speed belt-drive in 1980, followed by its reference tier TNT in 1986. The TNT evolved through the years, using a multiple-pulley or flywheel system to drive hefty lead, acrylic, and metal platters. These tables personified old-school American quality and helped establish VPI as a dominant turntable manufacturer for four decades. Even more telling is VPI's proximity to Thomas Edison's old factory in Menlo Park, New Jersey. How fitting it is, then, to counter the two decades of vinyl's so-called prostration to the compact disc with VPI's proof of Edison's endowment to analog perseverance.

4.44	TNT TURNTABLE, VPI, 1986
4.45–46	TNT MK.IV TURNTABLE, VPI, c.1997

4.44

4.45

4.46

○○   Eminent Technology

Founded in 1982 by Bruce Thigpen, Eminent Technology distinguished itself early on with its air-bearing turntables and tonearms. Its first product was the Model One, which established the foundation for its famous ET-2 in 1985, a collaborative effort with Edison Price. Both are examples of an air-bearing design in which "air pressure causes a hard coat of anodized aluminum spindle to float on a thin layer of air."[107] Along with Versa Dynamics, another 1980s proponent of air-bearing tonearms, Eminent Technology distinguished itself with this method and serves as one of its primary representatives.

4.47   ET-2 TONEARM, EMINENT TECHNOLOGY, 1985

4.47

○○ Fidelity Research Company

Established by Isamu Ikeda in 1964, Fidelity Research made tone-arms that have earned widespread collector status and are some of the more coveted vintage arms today. The FR-64, FR-64S, FR-66, and FR-66S arms were only available until 1984, when the company closed. Constructed with substantial mass in mind, these 9⅝-inch (24.5-centimeter) and 12-inch (30.5-centimeter) arms became popular for low-compliance moving-coil cartridges. Recognized for coil-spring dial-adjustable tracking force and simple rod-actuated anti-skating, the arms continue to be favored. Today the Japanese company Ikeda Sound Labs advances Fidelity Research's legacy designs.

| 4.48 | FR-66S TONEARM, FIDELITY RESEARCH, EARLY 1980s |
| 4.49 | FR-64S TONEARM, FIDELITY RESEARCH, c.1980 |

4.48

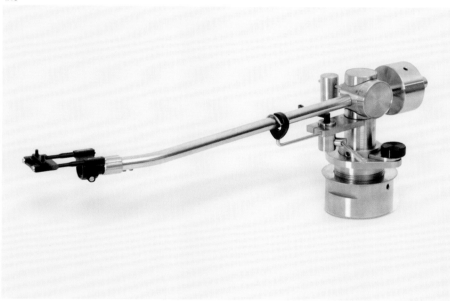

4.49

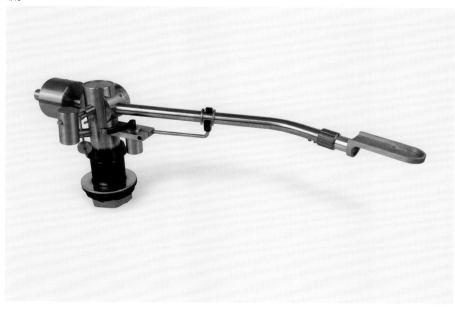

○○   Kiseki

In Japanese Kiseki means "miracle," and while the cartridge brand exudes exclusive Japanese artistry, it emanated in the 1980s from both Japanese and Dutch origins. Designed and built in Japan by Yoshiaki Sugano of Koetsu fame, the actual brand was the creation of Herman van den Dungen, an audio-industry veteran in the Netherlands. Later distancing himself from Sugano, van den Dungen had the Kiseki cartridges built in both Holland and Japan. The initial release was the Kiseki Blue, followed by the BlackHeart, PurpleHeart, Agate, and Lapis Lazuli, which were not dissimilar to Koetsu's exotic wood- and stone-body models. Kiseki continues to offer these prized moving-coil cartridges and maintains a dedicated following today.

4.50	AGATE CARTRIDGE, KISEKI, 1980s
4.51	BLUE CARTRIDGE, KISEKI, 1980s (THIS MODEL, BLUE N.O.S., 2011)
4.52	BLACKHEART CARTRIDGE, KISEKI, 1980s (THIS MODEL, BLACKHEART N.S., 2020)
4.53	PURPLEHEART CARTRIDGE, KISEKI, 1980s (THIS MODEL, PURPLEHEART N.S., 2015)

4.50

4.51

4.52

4.53

2000s

○○ The Analog Renaissance

The cover of this book features the 4000c turntable by Bang & Olufsen (B&O), an object that exemplifies 1970s culture shock, if not a complete reanimation of turntable design. Why choose the 4000c? Why does it lend itself to being the appointed emissary of the turntable arts? It would be easy to argue that its design merit speaks for itself, without having to explain the self-evident truth of its timelessness. But looks alone don't suffice, as these pages are full of examples of good design merging with analog technology.

In this case, the collaboration of Jacob Jensen (who defined his design philosophy as "different but not strange") with Karl Gustav Zeuthen and Villy Hansen yielded a turntable so strikingly different from conventional 1970s turntables that it came to define B&O's design mantra, along with waking up an industry that had grown complacent with the period's wooden plinths and industrial broadcast tanks.[108] Not dissimilar from the efforts of Dieter Rams of Braun, their work transitioned analog design from hobbyist-driven and myopic-audiophile realms into real-world living rooms and broader cultural acceptance.

In 2020, bridging five decades of analog continuity, B&O rereleased the 4000 series as a re-created limited edition. The painstaking restoration demonstrated a rejection of product obsolescence. In this case, a turntable from 1972 serves as a stark contrast to the short-lived and ephemeral gadgetry of Apple. This commitment to analog longevity occurred thirty-eight years after the first commercial compact disc (CD) was released, Billy Joel's *52nd Street*. Digital media is undoubtedly here to stay, but while CDs have been replaced by streaming in the 2000s, vinyl demonstrated resilience and a comeback that has enlivened the turntable-manufacturing apparatus.

This continuity into the 2000s does not rest with the efforts of B&O alone. Jochen Räke, for instance, codesigned the famous Michell turntables of the early 1970s and later formed his own Transrotor company. Transrotor is now a key contributor to analog design, with subtle and welcome cues to its Michell roots. Another notable example is Hideaki Nishikawa, the turntable pioneer who contributed to the legendary Micro Seiki and who is now behind TechDAS. Both Linn and Rega continue to manufacture their older designs, the LP12 and Planar 3, respectively, but with advanced reinterpretations. Technics's hegemony in the direct-drive DJ realm remains unchallenged, with the company expanding its range with even more ambitious and bespoke models. Brinkmann, VPI, and Thorens, along with other well-established turntable brands, continue to release new models that either reinterpret classic motifs or chart new courses for contemporary analog designs.

The market's renewed fascination with vinyl did not just awaken traditional brands; it simultaneously inspired new talents to emerge. With deference to past technological developments, a new breed of designers arose that advanced their forebears' achievements. In some cases, the more latent and hidden analog gems of the past have been unearthed and reformulated with fresh insights and technological know-how. Examples include: the evolution from the dual-arm-tube yet tangential-arm-inspired Burne Jones Super 90 tonearm to today's similarly designed Thales Simplicity arm; the more purist tangential arms from Versa Dynamics, Eminent Technology, Goldmund, and Souther Engineering; and contemporary linear trackers from Bergmann, Clearaudio, CSPort, Simon Yorke, and Walker. Breaking away from legendary Technics direct-drive motors is Wave Kinetics, forging ahead with its own direct-drive motor and application. Vertere's implementation of acrylic pays homage to the Oracle tables of the 1980s while TW Acustic has created a dedicated following around its copper platters. Wilson Benesch continues to evolve the use of carbon fiber, serving as inspiration for an industry now captivated with using that material for tonearms.

Similarly, the renewed appreciation for vintage designs has motivated Thorens to rerelease the TD 124 turntable roughly sixty-five years after the original legend was introduced. In Shindo Laboratory's curated refurbishment, the classic idler-drive Garrard 301, EMT tonearm, and Ortofon MC cartridge find modern interpretation, aiming for the ultimate recreation of classic tonal color and density. Reed takes it a step further in its hybrid idler-drive and belt-drive 3C turntable, allowing the user to switch between the attributes of the two drives.

Even the outliers have found their place in analog's renaissance, with 47 Labs and Kronos championing counter-rotating platters. Pivoted tonearm ingenuity and craftsmanship have taken on new heights, with Frank Schroeder, Graham, Ikeda, Marc Gomez, Moerch, and Rega taking strikingly divergent paths to achieve state-of-the-art designs.

Cartridge method has expanded exponentially, with Japan leading the world with legacy brands and new ones. Air Tight, Audio Note Japan, Audio-Technica, Dynavector, Fuuga, Hana, Kiseki, Koetsu, Lyra, My Sonic Labs, Murasakino, and Mutech have all revived Japan's great artistry in cartridge building. Countering the Japanese are European brands such as Jan Allaerts, Audio Note UK, Benz Micro, EMT, Ortofon, and Van den Hul. Grado serves American interests well, with its classic wood-body moving-coil (MC) cartridges, which have been in production for decades.

○○   The Resilience of Authenticity

New impulses come by regularly. At some point, that tried and tested playlist runs its course, spurring on the search for new music, taking us in potentially countless directions. It may be why many people prefer real-world digging, along with its built-in element of chance in a finite space. Some prefer a digital wormhole from the comfort of their home, which can be every bit as random. Vinyl-only, digital-only, cassette-only; today's world requires the mastery of many mediums. For some [reading] this issue, music is a largely private pursuit that finds its way into their work, while for others, music is something that needs to be shared immediately, either with friends or a crowd of dancers. More than anything, I think music is a reason to jump out of bed in the morning, a high that makes you shake your head in disbelief at the beauty held within a track you never knew existed until you put it on.[109]
—Karl Henkell, Editor-in-Chief, *Record* magazine, 2019

This quote exemplifies the musical inspiration for all that is analog—and in our case, its enduring agent, the delineative turntable. As representatives for the musical arts, both vinyl records and turntables foster a tactile and palpable connection with not just the artist but also the actual process of bringing the artist's work to life. Listening to recorded music using vinyl discs, turntables, tonearms, and cartridges undoubtedly requires more effort, especially when compared to simply streaming a song from the Internet. Yet humans have shown a fundamental desire for the experience of authenticity, regardless of the work needed to get there. In this sense, the continuous analog sine wave has proven indissoluble for those seeking the truth in music reproduction. And as long as this supernal resilience remains, so too will the turntable.

○○   47 Laboratory

Junji Kimura of 47 Labs stems from a select group of niche Japanese audio manufacturers emerging in the early 2000s. Straying from axiomatic designs and conventional thinking, Kimura's ideas even influenced Kronos in its current line of turntables. His defiance for mundane designs resulted in the Koma turntable, featuring two counter-rotating aluminum platters suspended by two powerful neodymium magnets. The concept is better explained by Kimura himself: "As for the effect of the counter-rotating platter, imagine a single platter turntable placed on a boat floating on calm water. No matter how we smooth out the friction of the rotation, we can not completely eliminate it, and given enough time, the force created by the rotation would be transmitted to the turntable base, to the boat, then to the water, making the boat rotate with the rotation of the platter and cause ripples on the water surface. The counter-rotating platter is [meant] to neutralize this force created by the primary platter."[110] Kimura's ingenuity did not stop at the Koma table, as his 4725 Tsurube tonearm also defied ordinary arm design: horizontal and vertical suspensions were placed in the arm pivot and in the middle, with the objective to improve tracking and reduce the tonearm's mass.

5.1–2   4724 KOMA TURNTABLE AND 4725 TSURUBE TONEARM, 47 LABS, 2012

5.1

5.2

○○ Swedish Analog Technologies (SAT)

What makes the 2000s analog revival so authentic are its newcomers. The old guard has unquestionably reemerged with renewed vigor, but the recent mavericks add cogency to the movement's pertinence. Marc Gomez of SAT, initially with tonearms and now with the introduction of the XD1 turntable, can certainly be counted as one of the key contributors to the recent movement. With a master of science degree in mechanical engineering, Gomez applies a great deal of this knowledge, specifically in the use of carbon fiber in his tonearms. The SAT tonearm features a unique application of carbon fiber that has been pre-impregnated, cured, and constructed as a monolithic tapered arm. Applying these engineering tools to the XD1 turntable, Gomez borrows the drive system from a Technics SP-10R but reinterprets it mechanically with a more robust motor housing and isolation. Utilizing a 33-pound (15-kilogram) vacuum-hold-down platter made of aged alloy, the XD1 also employs aged alloy for its chassis. Consistent with the effort to reduce vibrations, Gomez separates the motor controller in an external housing machined from a solid block of alloy. The extensive use of alloy lends to the solidity and unshakable form factor of the XD1.

| 5.3 | XD1 TURNTABLE, SAT, 2019 |

5.3

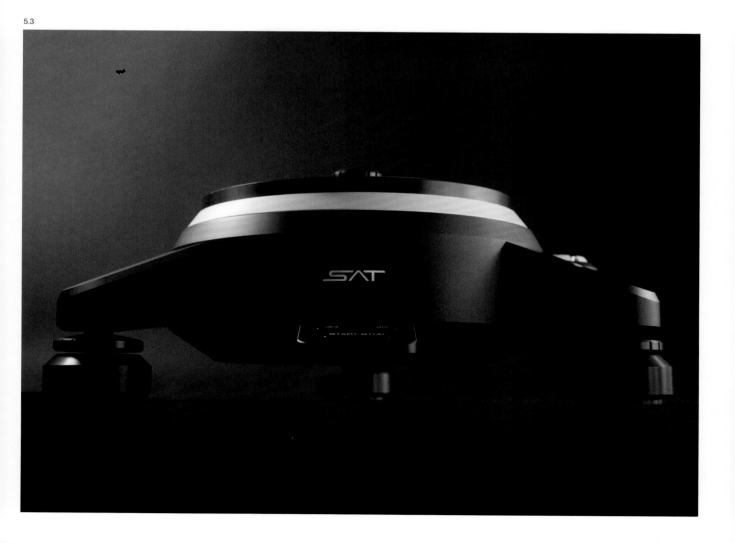

○○   Basis Audio

Founded by the U.S. industry veteran A. J. Conti, Basis turntables have represented a zealous commitment to analog design and application, as seen in its Transcendence turntable and SuperArm tonearm. Weighing 158 pounds (71.7 kilograms) with a single SuperArm tonearm, the mass-loaded and rigid-suspension turntable accommodates multiple tonearms of different lengths and features a sophisticated vacuum system, which refines the earlier efforts of predecessors (like air-suspended platters) in previous decades.

| 5.4 | TRANSCENDENCE TURNTABLE AND SUPERARM TONEARM, BASIS, 2017 |
| 5.5 | INSPIRATION TURNTABLE AND VECTOR TONEARM, BASIS, 2012 |

5.4

5.5

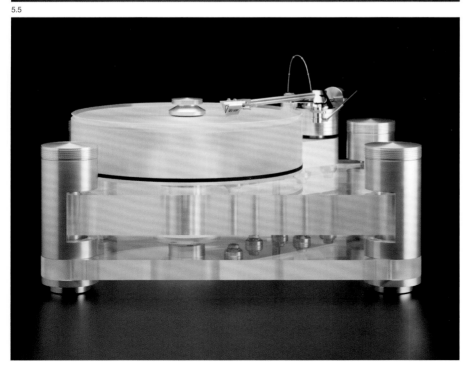

○○ Acoustic Signature

Founded in 1996 by Gunther Frohnhoefer, this German company has since become an established turntable and tonearm manufacturer. Joining the ranks of other extreme precision-engineered tables, Acoustic Signature has taken its design ethos a step further by utilizing multiple motors. For instance, the Invictus Neo model has six integrated, completely insulated AC motors. The intent with multiple motors is to create a high-torque device with consistent speed. Acoustic Signature additionally employs a massive amount of aluminum in its chassis for resonance and vibration control.

5.6–7   ASCONA NEO TURNTABLE, ACOUSTIC SIGNATURE, 2020

5.6

5.7

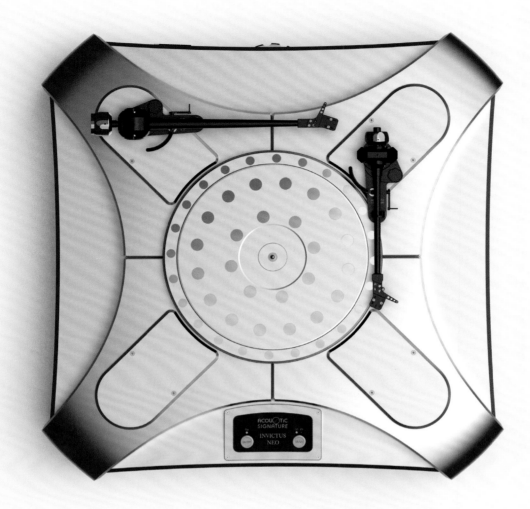

5.8

5.9

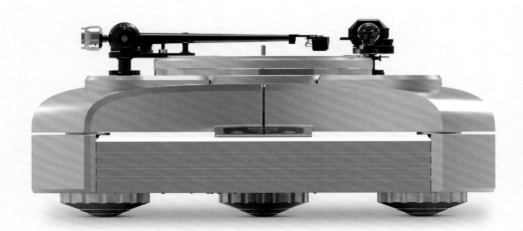

○○   Döhmann

Long before Mark Döhmann's contribution to Continuum Audio Lab's Caliburn turntable, the aeronautics engineer was fascinated by analog reproduction and its mechanical possibilities. By 2011 Döhmann's collaborative talents led him to Frank Schroeder and Rumen Artarski. Together they designed the Döhmann company's first turntable, Helix One, and the Schroeder CB tonearm. Applying technologies from the fields of medical imaging, electron microscopy, nanotechnology measurement, and aerospace design, the Helix One represented a tour de force of applied sciences in relation to analog design. This was particularly evident in its isolation and resonance-control systems. In 2018, owing to his contribution to turntable design, Mark Döhmann received a "Lifetime Achievement Award for Services to Analogue and Industry" from *Sound and Vision* magazine.[111]

5.11   HELIX ONE MK2 TURNTABLE, DÖHMANN, 2019

5.11

○○   Analog Manufaktur Germany (AMG)

The Bavarian company AMG, founded by Werner Röschlau, entered the arena in 2011, quickly gaining devotees for its quality of sound and elegant designs. AMG pioneered a two-point tonearm-bearing mechanism made of spring steel; this is implemented into its current 9W and 12J tonearms. Its turntables have been compared by the press to Leica cameras in terms of AMG's attention to precision craftsmanship and finely machined components. AMG's minimalist and sparse push-button controls belie the engineering that goes into its designs, especially its Viella and Giro models. Early on, the firm adopted aircraft-grade aluminum for the chassis—perhaps due to Röschlau's background in aeronautical engineering—along with a Lorenzi motor, prized for its sintered bronze bearings, which are self-lubricating.

5.12   V12 TURNTABLE, AMG, 2010

5.12

5.13
5.14

5.15

5.16

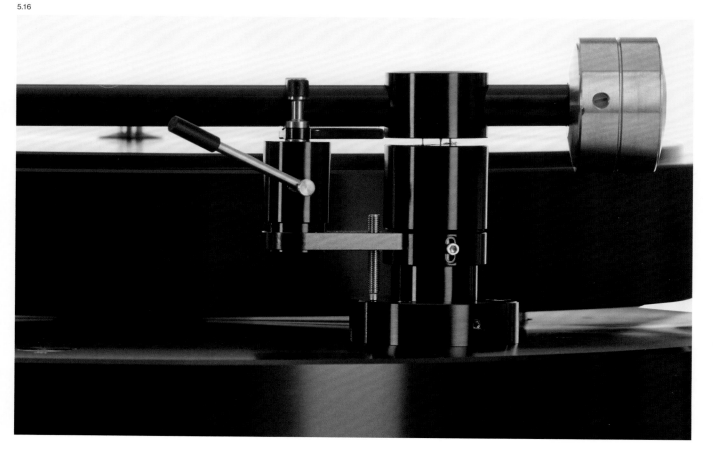

○○ Kronos

Creating one of the most visually compelling designs of the 2000s is the Canadian company Kronos. Picking up where Junji Kimura left off with his Koma turntable, Kronos similarly engages two counter-rotating platters, each weighing 30 pounds (13.6 kilograms), all in the effort to reduce vibration, resonance, and mechanical noise. A great deal of effort is also applied toward speed stability with Kronos's DC-computer speed controller and mass-loaded stable plinth.

5.17	KRONOS PRO TURNTABLE, KRONOS, 2012
5.18	SPARTA TURNTABLE, KRONOS, 2013

5.17

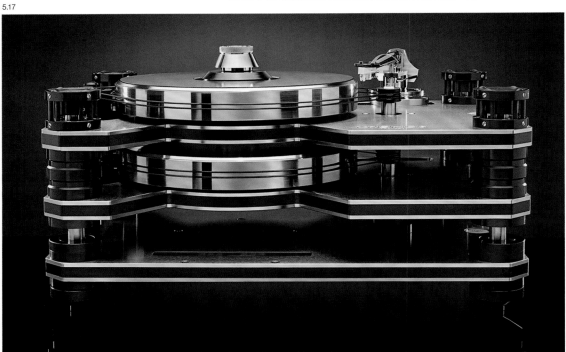

5.18

○○ Bergmann

It is no small coincidence that much of the current analog renaissance flows from Denmark, a country rich in audio-design history. The most visible representative of the country's analog roots is Bang & Olufsen; this is especially evident when one considers the company's varied turntables and iconic mid-century form factor. But brands such as Duelund, Gryphon, Jantzen, Horning, and Vitus have all contributed to validating the country's analog standing. Within this breeding ground, the mechanical engineer Johnnie Bergmann founded his company in 2008, releasing its first turntable, the Sindre. Bergmann has applied his engineering knowledge and tools to air-bearing tables and air-bearing tangential tonearms. The air-bearing Galder model currently reflects Bergmann's state-of-the-art aspirations with an air-cushioned floating platter, thereby avoiding mechanical-bearing noise.

5.19   GALDER TURNTABLE, BERGMANN, 2017

5.19

5.20

5.21

5.22

5.23

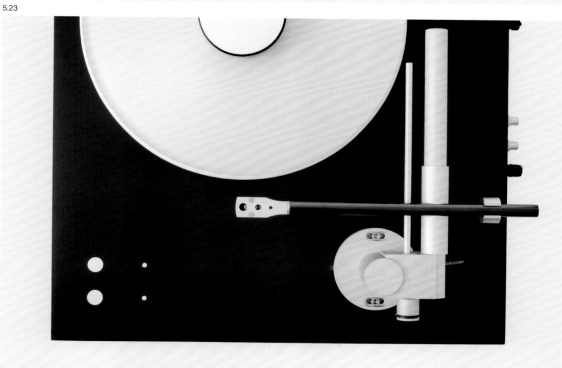

○○ Continuum Audio Labs

The Australian company Continuum introduced a novel concept to the analog field. Traditionally, solo designers handled all aspects of designing a turntable; design has generally not developed as a collaborative effort but more often materialized from an individual's autonomous vision. Seeing this individualistic approach as an obstacle to turntable development, Continuum enlisted a design team early on, with each member contributing a unique skill set. In 2005, with a primary team consisting of the lead engineer Mark Döhmann along with Joe Persico and Michael Baribas, Continuum released the tri-chassis Caliburn turntable and Cobra tonearm. The ambitiously engineered vacuum-platter turntable was hailed as a game changer, especially for its unique suspension, which decoupled it from its surroundings. Years later and with a new design team, the high-mass and plinth-less Obsidian model utilizes creative metallurgy in its generous application of tungsten, in addition to an isolated motor on independent mounts.

5.24	CALIBURN TURNTABLE AND COBRA TONEARM, CONTINUUM, 2005
5.25	OBSIDIAN TURNTABLE AND VIPER TONEARM, CONTINUUM, 2016

5.24

5.25

○○   Clearaudio

Founded by Peter Suchy in 1978, Clearaudio first released a moving-coil (MC) cartridge, becoming known as a premier supplier of high-end MC cartridges during high-end audio's ascent in the 1970s and 1980s. The company collaborated with Goldmund to create the Clearaudio Goldmund MC cartridge, which was often partnered with Goldmund's T3 tonearm. Transitioning to turntable production, Clearaudio today represents one of the world's dominant entities, with a vast range of models. Yet contributing to the company's analog status was not its turntables but rather its early embrace of the classic tangential tonearm by Souther Engineering. In the 1980s Clearaudio purchased the Boston-based Souther and its Tri-Quartz (TQ) tangential-tonearm technology.[112] Still in production, the Clearaudio Souther TQ-1 is a refinement of the original design, now titled the Statement TT1.

| 5.26–27 | STATEMENT V2 TURNTABLE AND TT1-MI TONEARM, CLEARAUDIO, 2016 [BELOW AND OVERLEAF, LEFT] |
| 5.28 | MASTER INNOVATION TURNTABLE WITH TT1-MI TONEARM AND OLYMPUS STAND, CLEARAUDIO, c.2014 [OVERLEAF, RIGHT] |

5.26

○○   CSPort

Throughout the preceding decades, Japan held an estimable place in evolving turntable design. Examples from Micro Seiki, Nakamichi, and Technics set the bar high for advancing the country's analog skill set. But by the 1990s, only Technics remained, holding the torch for Japan's turntable legacy—albeit more culturally mainstream than the extreme analog dynamism of the past. In terms of Japan's industry of high-end design, all talents were drawn toward digital, and for years, the dearth of analog seemed to dictate the future. But with vinyl's recovery, Japan has reemerged as a formidable player. Along with the Japanese entity TechDAS, CSPort has resurrected high-mass tables, air-floating platters, and air-floating tangential tonearms. The vanguard design of the LFT1M2 is perfect proof of this effort, with a 220-pound (99.8-kilogram) granite base, a floating platter that rotates by inertia alone, an air-float linear-tracking tonearm, and a medical-grade air pump that supplies the platter and arm. In an effort to reduce friction, CSPort uses a thin thread for its belt, as opposed to the industry's standard material of rubber.

5.29   TAT2M2 TURNTABLE, CSPORT, c.2021

5.30–31   LFT1M2 TURNTABLE SYSTEM, CSPORT, c.2021

5.29

5.30

5.31

○○　DaVinciAudio Labs

Another recently emerging Swiss firm is DaVinciAudio Labs, founded by Peter Brem. Acclaimed by the press as one of "the highest-fidelity turntables and tonearms in the world," its Reference turntable helped establish DaVinci as a principal player in Switzerland's newly flourishing turntable industry.[113] With four tonearm bases, the current iteration Reference MKII weighs 364 pounds (165.1 kilograms) and addresses vibrations with its silent magnet-bearing technology, separate motor and control unit, and integrated platter-damping system. Adding to the brand's exclusivity is its limited-edition Reference model (with only seventy-seven pieces produced) finished in Aston Martin Onyx Black, which hosts two tonearms.

5.32

5.33

○○   Wilson Benesch

Few companies stand for such analog conviction as Wilson Benesch. In 1989 when turntables were routinely abandoned on curbsides, the young British firm arose by proffering a business plan to the Department of Trade and Industry in Her Majesty's Government. The plan argued that the vinyl record was preferable to the compact disc as a music format and that new advanced materials were available to create a viable and unique new product in the marketplace. With the grant approved, Wilson Benesch was formed and immediately released its eponymous first turntable. What made this table so innovative and groundbreaking was the use of carbon fiber to construct its sub-chassis, the first instance of this material being implemented in a turntable design.[114] With increased knowledge in the application of carbon fiber, Wilson Benesch introduced the A.C.T. tonearm constructed of the material. Nearly thirty years later, the company continues to employ carbon fiber in its current A.C.T. 25 tonearm. The myriad turntable and tonearm designs incorporating carbon fiber collectively owe a debt of gratitude to Wilson Benesch for pioneering the material's appositeness and application for analog instruments.

5.34   CIRCLE 25 TURNTABLE AND A.C.T. 25 TONEARM, WILSON BENESCH, 2014

5.34

○○   De Baer

Like Japan, Switzerland also experienced a decline of its once-formidable analog apparatus. As the 1990s progressed, Goldmund and Revox were no longer supplying turntables. Thorens, although still producing tables, had lost much of its market presence and cache, and the once-great Lenco was all but a prehistoric memory. What remained in Switzerland during the ensuing years was a vibrant high-end audio sector, devoid of any analog development. Not surprisingly, with the country's rich history in turntable craft, it has recently reemerged as a hot spot for modern analog ingenuity. One entity continuing Switzerland's traditions is De Baer, a company that was formed by Kurt Baer and developed its first turntable in 2013. With assistance from Jetmax, a precision engineering company, De Baer tables and tonearms have demonstrated a very high degree of technical sophistication, complemented by the company's monolithic stone-based designs. De Baer places a great deal of emphasis on decoupling its platter bearing and tonearm base from the chassis by way of hardened steel balls. Magnetic drive is employed, resulting in a floating platter. De Baer's dual carbon-fiber tonearm further demonstrates a comprehensive approach and cutting-edge vision for this new Swiss brand.

5.35   TOPAS 12-09 TURNTABLE AND ONYX TONEARM, DE BAER, 2018

5.35

5.36

5.37

5.38

5.39

○○   Reed

The Lithuania-based firm is the vision of Vidmantas Triukas, a former radio engineer, with patents concerning the acoustical noise of plasma in long-range ballistic missiles. Turning his talents to more peaceful applications, Triukas has created one of the most innovative turntable companies of the 2000s. Reed's Muse 3C model is a testament to the company's creativity, as the table implements both friction-drive (as in the Garrard 301) and belt-drive mechanisms. By simply replacing the traction rollers and placing a belt, a user can switch between either drive system, depending on subjective sonic preferences.

| 5.40 | MUSE 3C TURNTABLE, REED, MID-2010s |
| 5.41 | MUSE 1C TURNTABLE, REED, MID-2010s |

5.40

5.41

OO   Rega

Founded in 1973 and based in the United Kingdom, Rega may be considered one of the most enduring turntable manufacturers into the 2000s. It is primarily influential for its Planar 3 model, introduced in 1977 and still produced today. The remarkable ascent of Rega in analog circles was neither due to maximal aesthetic designs nor high-end exotic verbiage. Rather the company broke the compliant-suspension mold set by companies such as Acoustic Research, Linn, and Thorens in favor of a lightweight but rigid solid plinth. Resting on rubber feet, Rega's suspension-less and belt-driven design became synonymous with excellent sound and British value. Creating and defining the niche of high-quality and value-driven turntable designs, Rega has earned a lasting reputation along with accolades throughout the years: "Few hi-fi components have lived longer or exerted greater influence than Rega's Planar 3 turntable."[115]

5.42   PLANAR 3 TURNTABLE, REGA, 1977 (THIS MODEL, 2016)

5.42

5.43

5.44

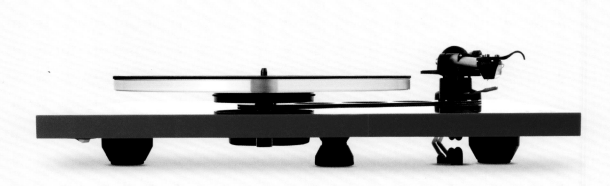

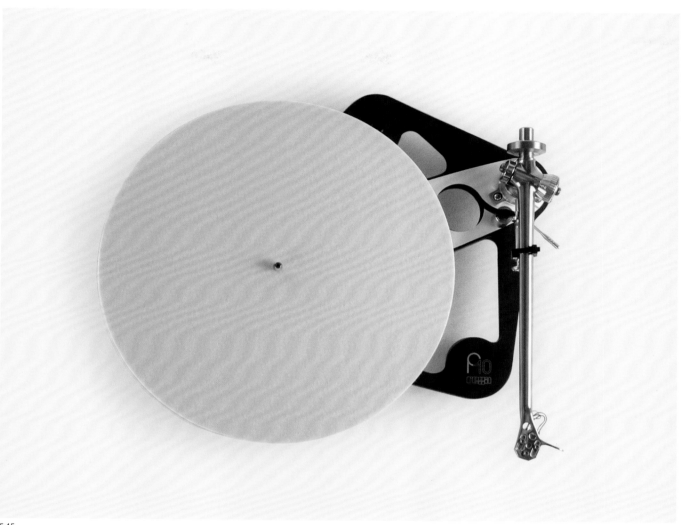

5.45
5.46

○○ Shindo Laboratory

Along with Thorens, Technics, and various other classics, the Garrard 301 has become one of the most coveted and restored turntables during analog's revival. Undoubtedly helpful is the fecund supply of Garrard restoration outfits and specialty craftspeople. Yet in the niche world of Garrard 301 restorations, Shindo of Japan has redefined the possibilities inherent in this idler-drive classic. In this vein, Shindo modifies the bearing for smoother operation and supplies a solid-wood layered and laminated plinth and custom platter. In addition, Shindo refashions to its specifications an EMT twelve-inch tonearm and Ortofon stereo pickup. With such a comprehensive approach, Shindo attempts to attain a thorough reinterpretation of the venerable Garrard 301.

5.47   301 TURNTABLE, GARRARD, RESTORED AND UPGRADED BY SHINDO, c.2010

5.47

○○   Simon Yorke Designs

The new millennium introduced one of the most eccentric and talented turntable designers, Simon Yorke. First blueprinting his sculpted Aeroarm air-bearing tangential tonearm in 1985, he has since refined it, claiming the following about its impetus: "The Aeroarm is not for the faint-hearted. It is not a 'fit and forget' device. It was neither designed as a 'product' nor propaganda of promises. It will not buy you time nor ease your life. Indeed, it may drive you crazy... So, what is it? The Aeroarm is a sonic microscope, an instrument for extracting information stored in analog record grooves. It does this without judgment, simply 'doing what it says on the tin' without flattery, prejudice, or desire."[116] Implicit in Yorke's facetious but well-meaning description is a vision of retrieving brutal truth in vinyl replay. This philosophy underlies all of his turntables as well and perhaps accounts for his most noteworthy client: the United States Library of Congress, which uses a Simon York turntable to archive history's vinyl repository.

| 5.48 | S10 TURNTABLE AND AEROARM TONEARM, SIMON YORKE, c.2010 |
| 5.49 | S9 VERSION 3 (PURE) TURNTABLE, SIMON YORKE, 2020 |

5.48

5.49

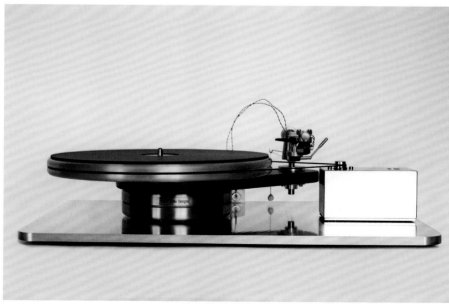

○○   Sperling

Within the realm of colossal turntable design, Sperling has emerged with a prominent example of the genre. But weight and presence alone do not define its reference L-1 turntable. Unique to Sperling is a selection of different inlay materials for the platter, permitting a user to achieve different tonal attributes. Based on subjective listening preferences, various materials may be used, such as wenge wood, Portuguese argillaceous shale, or acrylic. Sperling seems to attach great importance to user adjustability as it additionally provides a belt tensioner, which permits fine on-the-fly adjustments of the belt, which, like the platter inlays, allows for different tonal characteristics.

5.50   L-1 TURNTABLE, SPERLING, 2013

5.50

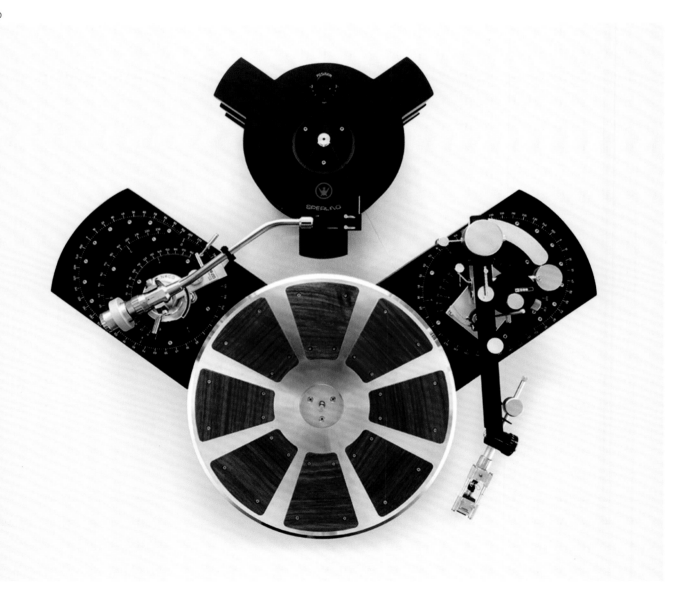

○○   Wave Kinetics

Another leading-edge turntable in the 2000s is the Wave Kinetics NVS Reference. To its credit, and distinguishing it from other entities that simply employ the Technics motor, Wave Kinetics has bravely developed its own laboratory-grade direct-drive system. In addition to its motor-control system, Wave Kinetics applies a great deal of thought to vibration attenuation. With a specially tuned platform to support the table, a dense chassis constructed from solid-metal billets and internal resonance-control damping devices, the NVS has garnered praise for its innovative approach to analog methods.

5.51   NVS REFERENCE TURNTABLE, WAVE KINETICS, c.2011

5.51

○○   Transrotor

This company was founded in 1976 by the mechanical engineer Jochen Räke, who developed his turntable acumen while contributing to the designs of Michell turntables in the early 1970s. Such a pedigree has contributed to Transrotor's primacy on the analog front. Adventuring into acrylic designs in the 1970s, along with its pioneering efforts in magnetic, frictionless bearings, Transrotor developed strong brand loyalty. Carrying on into the 2000s, Transrotor's latest free-magnetic-drive bearing technology, which magnetically couples the motor to the platter, is evident in the firm's aluminum and acrylic masterpiece, the Tourbillon FMD. With up to three motors and an inverted hydrodynamic oil-fed bearing, the Tourbillon lives up to Transrotor's technical legacy, with visual cues from the original Michell designs.

5.52–53   TOURBILLON FMD TURNTABLE, TRANSROTOR, 2006 [BELOW AND OPPOSITE]

5.52

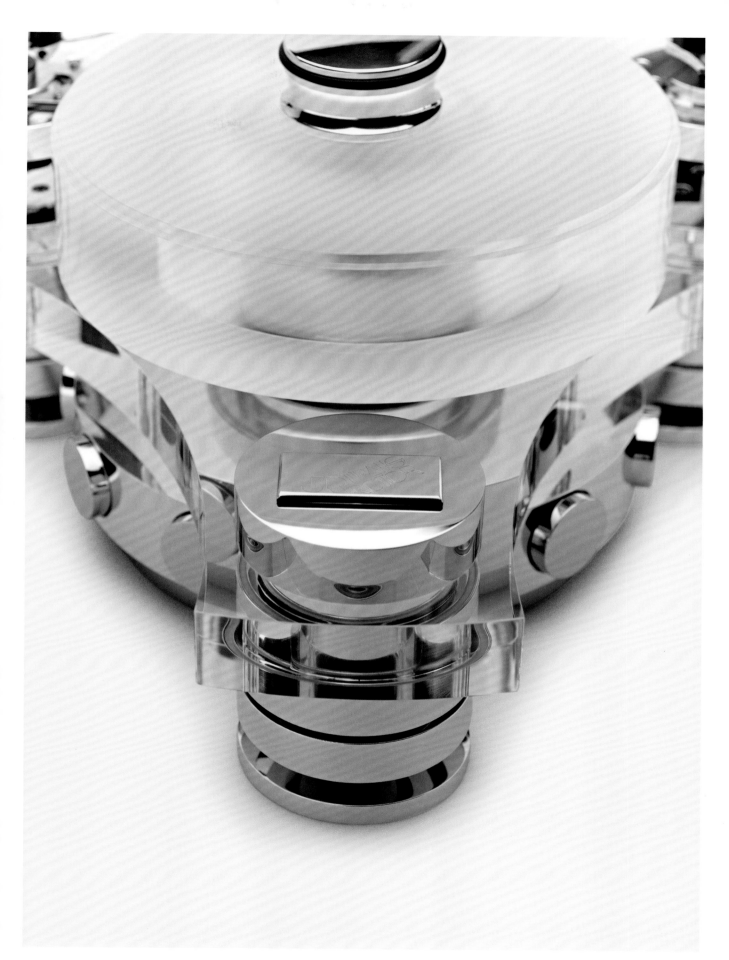

5.54

5.55

5.56

5.57

○○ TechDAS

As the manager of Micro Seiki's technical department in the 1980s, Hideaki Nishikawa oversaw the development of the ambitious SX-8000 along with other seminal products for the venerable brand. In 2010 he founded TechDAS, which built upon Micro Seiki's innovations, primarily relating to vacuum seals, to hold down records, and air-bearing platters. For the Air Force Zero model, TechDAS taps into the merits of the (now rare) vintage Papst motor formerly used in tape recorders. Nishikawa embellishes the three-phase twelve-pole synchronous motor with an air-bearing and flywheel mechanism, which drives the high-torque motor. Implementing a Papst motor is not the only vintage element inspiring the Air Force Zero, as the table size is determined by the standard set by the classic EMT 927 turntable of the 1950s.

| 5.58 | AIR FORCE ZERO TURNTABLE, TECHDAS, 2019 |
| 5.59 | AIR FORCE III PREMIUM TURNTABLE, TECHDAS, 2017 |

5.58

5.59

5.60

5.61

○○   Thales (HiFiction AG)

There is no doubt about Switzerland's contribution to the analog arts. The country's history is rich with examples, but with the renewed global interest in vinyl, firms such as Benz Micro, De Baer, and DaVinci have put Switzerland back on the map. One newcomer, however, has arrived at a position of analog preeminence. Influencing all aspects of vinyl playback, Thales builds turntables, tonearms, cartridges, and phono stages. Expanding even further, in 2018 it assumed control over EMT cartridges, continuing the great legacy of this storied analog firm. Led by Micha Huber, Thales in 2005 initially tapped into the precedence established by the Burne Jones Super 90 tangential tonearm from the late 1950s. Thales's first tonearm was not a purely tangential arm; it can more accurately be described as a pivoted arm with tangential tracking. The philosophy adheres to the theorem known as Thales's circle, which outlines the geometry to construct a tangent. In the realm of turntable design, Thales's svelte and minimalist TTT-Compact II features a unique friction-drive and belt-drive mechanism via two pulleys and three flywheels.

5.62–64   TTT-COMPACT II TURNTABLE AND STATEMENT TONEARM, THALES, 2016

5.62

5.63

5.64

○○   TW Acustic

In many instances, a brand's importance and relevance cannot be explained by specifications alone. The 2000s introduced a new German brand whose merits can be better understood by the record collectors and vinyl devotees who own it. In the deep realm of serious vinyl collecting, Jeffrey Catalano, a notable New York–based record collector, chooses TW Acustic as his reference tool. Perhaps this is due to the company's generous application of copper in the 66-pound (29.9-kilogram) platter of its Raven Black Night turntable or the model's unique three-motor mechanism with machined drive belt. Details like a bronze tonearm board and bearing may also account for its fidelity, helping to explain its following among vinyl mavens.

| 5.65 | RAVEN AC TURNTABLE, TW ACUSTIC, 2006 |
| 5.66 | RAVEN BLACK NIGHT TURNTABLE, TW ACUSTIC, 2009 |

5.65

5.66

○○   Walker

Acclaimed by the press as the "granddaddy of all high-end turntables," the Walker Proscenium Black Diamond turntable entered the fray in the 1990s, just in time to peak during vinyl's eventual resurgence.[117] Now in its MK VI iteration, the 240-pound (108.9-kilogram) monument of turntable design features a "specially treated, fine-grained crystalline material that reduces static build-up and cancels the effect of virtually all EMI, RFI, and micro-waves [and] is employed at strategic locations in the turntable's operation."[118] Typical of the company's approach is an air-bearing platter and air-bearing tangential tonearm, along with a massive application of dense marble for the base and separate motor-control unit. Despite a reference turntable arena replete with copious examples, the Proscenium remains a monument of turntable design and execution, earning it the accolade as one of the most significant turntables of all time.[119]

5.67   PROSCENIUM BLACK DIAMOND VI MASTER REFERENCE TURNTABLE, WALKER, 2021

5.67

○○ Vertere

With his UK-based Roksan brand, the veteran turntable designer Touraj Moghaddam rose to analog fame in the 1980s and 1990s. Roksan turntables, most famously the Xerxes model, developed a global following and served as a fierce competitor to Linn's LP12.[120] By the 2000s Moghaddam transitioned to his new company, Vertere, and has once again challenged analog convention. Moghaddam's close connection to the music industry has given him access to master tapes, which he then compares to the sound produced by his turntables. Applying these tools to the reference RG-1 model, Vertere employs a precision main bearing, consisting of an aerospace-grade phosphor bronze housing and a super-precision tungsten-carbide spindle, along with a silicon-nitride ball and a two-piece nonresonant alloy and acrylic platter. The suspension suggests a well-planned hybrid approach, with its three-stage compliant and two-stage rigid applications. In an interview, when asked how the record player of 2040 would differ from that of 2020, Moghaddam responded: "A 2040 record player would most likely be powered by an exercise bike or some 'green' energy equipment—self-powering, maybe by a wind turbine? That would be great, as it would definitely keep me in business, if I'm still alive."[121]

| 5.68 | RG-1 TURNTABLE, VERTERE, c.2015 |
| 5.69–70 | SG-1 TURNTABLE, VERTERE, c.2015 |

5.68

5.69

5.70

○○ Frank Schroeder

For roughly three decades, Germany's Frank Schroeder has been crafting tonearms for analog enthusiasts. With a background in precision watchmaking, Schroeder has spent a great deal of time thinking about how to reduce bearing friction by way of engaging neodymium magnets, thereby achieving the lowest attrition possible. Universally admired for their sheer beauty, Schroeder's graceful creations have reintroduced classic German design to an analog field littered with austere metallic examples.

5.71   NO. 2 TONEARM, FRANK SCHROEDER, 2012

5.71

○○   Jan Allaerts

Founded in 1978, the Belgium-based company Jan Allaerts can be considered the European equivalent of Japan's artisanal-period Supex or Koetsu. Meticulously crafting each cartridge by hand, Allaerts mills and drills the cases along with gold-coating them. But one of the key features of Allaerts cartridges is their coil windings. In the case of the MC2 Formula One moving-coil cartridge, Allaerts carefully hand-winds 20-micron-thick gold wire. Further refining its designs, Allaerts employs a highly polished FG-S high-tech diamond tip.

| 5.72 | MC1 ECO CARTRIDGE, JAN ALLAERTS, 2000s |
| 5.73 | MC2 FORMULA ONE CARTRIDGE, JAN ALLAERTS, 2000s |

5.72

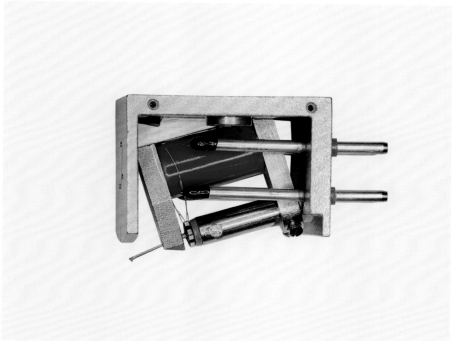

5.73

○○   Koetsu

With his credentials already established with Supex, Yoshiaki Sugano formed Koetsu in the early 1980s, naming the company after the Japanese artist Hon'ami Koetsu. The company's reverence toward cartridge form underlies its mission. Early on, Sugano championed the use of rare platinum-iron magnets, high-purity 6N copper, and exotic wood and stone bodies. Yoshiaki's son Fumihiko apprenticed under his father and continues his traditions into the 2000s. For instance, the Urushi Tsugaru in current production is hand-lacquered in the traditional *urushi* method, said to date back nine thousand years. Embellishing this artisanal heirloom even further, Fumihiko applies silver to its copper coils and seeks out stones such as onyx, jade, rhodonite, and coral stone for its housings.

5.74	URUSHI TSUGARU CARTRIDGE WITH ROSEWOOD BODY, KOETSU, 2000s
5.75	RHODONITE CARTRIDGE, KOETSU, 2000s
5.76	JADE PLATINUM CARTRIDGE, KOETSU, 2000s

5.74

5.75

5.76

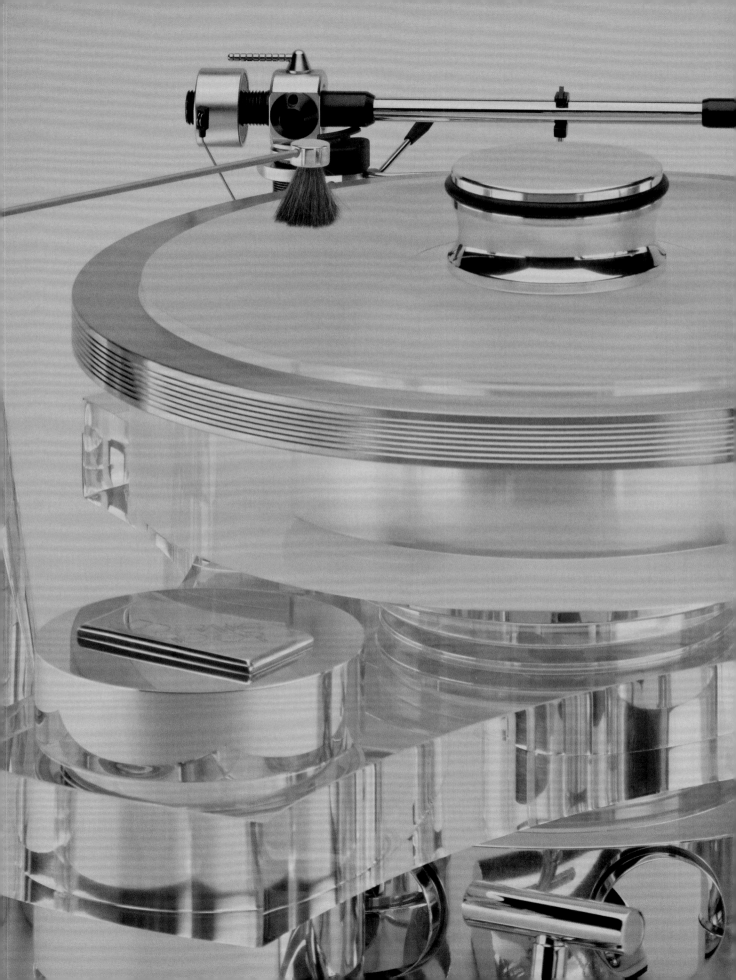

1 Alec Macfarlane and Chie Kobayashi, "Vinyl Comeback: Sony to Produce Records Again After 28-Year Break," *CNN Money*, June 30, 2017, money.cnn.com/2017/06/30/news/sony-music-brings-back-vinyl-records/index.html.

2 Noah Yoo, "Vinyl Outsells CDs For the First Time in Decades," *Pitchfork*, September 10, 2020, pitchfork.com/news/vinyl-outsells-cds-for-the-first-time-in-decades.

3 For readers seeking an academically comprehensive history of the recording and music industry, I recommend one of my favorite sources: Greg Milner, *Perfecting Sound Forever: An Aural History of Recorded Music* (Macmillan, 2010).

4 B. C. Forbes, "Why Do So Many Men Never Amount to Anything? (Interview with Thomas A. Edison)," *American Magazine* 91 (January 1921).

5 Tom Everett, "Writing Sound with a Human Ear: Reconstructing Bell and Blake's 1874 Ear Phonautograph," *Science Museum Group Journal*, no. 12 (Autumn 2019), dx.doi.org/10.15180/191206.

6 Thomas L. Hankins and Robert J. Silverman, *Instruments and the Imagination* (Princeton University Press, 1995), 133–35.

7 Patrick Feaster, "The Phonautographic Manuscripts of Édouard-Léon Scott de Martinville," *FirstSounds.org*, 2010, 1–81, www.firstsounds.org/publications/articles/Phonautographic-Manuscripts.pdf.

8 Ibid.

9 Merrill Fabry, "What Was the First Sound Ever Recorded by a Machine?" *Time*, May 1, 2018, time.com/5084599/first-recorded-sound.

10 Steven E. Schoenherr, "Leon Scott and the Phonautograph," *Recording Technology History*, www.aes-media.org/historical/html/recording.technology.history/scott.html.

11 Jody Rosen, "Researchers Play Tune Recorded Before Edison," *New York Times*, March 27, 2008, www.nytimes.com/2008/03/27/arts/27soun.html.

12 Ibid.

13 Chronomedia, "1875–1879," *Terra Media*, www.terramedia.co.uk/Chronomedia/years/1875-1879.htm.

14 Robin Doak, "The Phonograph," *World Almanac Library*, 2006, 7.

15 David J. Steffen, *From Edison to Marconi: The First Thirty Years of Recorded Music*, (McFarland, 2014), 23.

16 Ibid., 24.

17 Timothy Dowd, "Culture and Commodification: Technology and Structural Power in the Early US Recording Industry," *International Journal of Sociology and Social Policy* 22, nos. 1/2/3: 106–40, doi.org/10.1108/01443330210789979.

18 Timothy Fabrizio, "The Graphophone in Washington D.C.," *ARSC Journal* 27, no. 1 (1996).

19 Bill Pratt, "The Development Of Cylinder Records—Part 3," *Antique Phonograph News*, February 1985, www.capsnews.org/apn1985-2.htm.

20 Peter Tschmuck, *Creativity and Innovation in the Music Industry* (Springer Science and Business Media, 2006), 7.

21 T. F. Gregory, "The iPod and the Gramophone," *AAPLinvestors.net*, December 19, 2006, aaplinvestors.net/stats/ipod/ipodgramophone.

22 "V is for Victrola Record Players: The History of the Famous Gramophones That Entertained Millions," *Click Americana*, clickamericana.com/media/music/v-is-for-victrola-record-players-the-history-of-the-gramophones-that-entertained-millions.

23 "The Nipper Saga," *Design Boom*, web.archive.org/web/20150924073551/http://www.designboom.com/history/nipper.html.

24 "RCA Red Seal Records Explained," *Everything Explained Today*, everything.explained.today/RCA_Red_Seal_Records.

25 Frank Hoffmann and Howard Ferstler, *The Encyclopedia of Recorded Sound* (CRC Press, 2005).

26 Hoffman and Ferstler, 531.

27 "It all started with Emil Berliner," *Emil Berliner Studios*, emil-berliner-studios.com/en/history.

28 Paul Vernon, "Odeon Records: Their 'Ethnic' Output," *Musical Traditions*, July 31, 1997, www.mustrad.org.uk/articles/odeon.htm.

29 Howard Rye, "Odeon Records," in *The New Grove Dictionary of Jazz*, vol. 3, 2nd ed., ed. Barry Kernfeld (New York: Grove's Dictionaries, 2002), 184.

30 Vernon.

31 Hugo Strotbaum, ed., "The Fred Gaisberg Diaries, Part 2: Going East (1902–1903)," *Recording Pioneers*, 2010, www.recordingpioneers.com/docs/GAISBERG_DIARIES_2.pdf.

32 Nausika, "Sound Storing Machines—The First 78rpm Records from Japan, 1903– 1912: Early Recorded Japanese Music Still Sounding Fresh After Over 100 Years," *The Sound Projector*, April 9, 2021, www.thesoundprojector.com/2021/04/09/sound-storing-machines-the-first-78rpm-records-from-japan-1903-1912.

33 Maria Popova, "In Praise of Shadows: Ancient Japanese Aesthetics and Why Every Technology Is a Technology of Thought," *Brain Pickings*, May 28, 2015, www.brainpickings.org/2015/05/28/in-praise-of-shadows-tanizaki.

34 "VV-280," *The Victor-Victrola Page*, www.victor-victrola.com/280.htm.

35 *The Talking Machine World* 20, no. 9, worldradiohistory.com/Archive-Talking-Machine/20s/Talking-Machine-1924-09.pdf; Simon Frith, *Popular Music: Music and Society* (Psychology Press, 2004).

36 Matthew Mooney, "Music That Scared America: The Early Days of Jazz," *Lessons in US History* (Regents of the University of California, 2006), cpb-us-e2.wpmucdn.com/sites.uci.edu/dist/5/2530/files/2016/03/11.5-HOT-Early_Days_of_Jazz.pdf.

37 Rick Kennedy, *Jelly Roll, Bix, and Hoagy: Gennett Studios and the Birth of Recorded Jazz* (Indiana University, 1994), 141.

38 "The Rise and Fall of Black Swan Records," *Radio Diaries*, www.radiodiaries.org/black-swan-records.

39 "A Quick History of the Victor Phonograph," *The Victor-Victrola Page*, www.victor-victrola.com/History%20of%20the%20Victor%20Phonograph.htm.

40 Roland Gelatt, *The Fabulous Phonograph: 1877–1977* (New York: MacMillan, 1954).

41 "The History, Working, and Applications of Vacuum Tubes," *Science Struck*, sciencestruck.com/vacuum-tube-applications.

42 "Lee de Forest," *Britannica*, www.britannica.com/biography/Lee-de-Forest.

43 "Lee de Forest Invents the Triode, the First Widely Used Electronic Device That Can Amplify," *History of Information*, www.historyofinformation.com/detail.php?id=563.

44 Paul J. Nahin, *Oliver Heaviside: The Life, Work, and Times of an Electrical Genius of the Victorian Age* (JHU Press, 2002), 67; Anton Huurdeman, *The Worldwide History of Telecommunications* (John Wiley & Sons, 2003), 178.

45 Hugh Robjohns, "A Brief History of Microphones," *Microphone Data* (Microphone

Data Ltd., 2010), microphone-data.com/media/filestore/articles/History-10.pdf.

46 Ernest Newman, *Sunday Times*, July 11, 1926.

47 "New Music Machine Thrills All Hearers At First Test Here," *New York Times*, October 7, 1925, 1.

48 "Jack Kapp, Headed Decca Records, 47; Founder of Company in 1933 Dies–Crosby, Jolson and Other Stars on His List," *New York Times*, March 26, 1949, www.nytimes.com/1949/03/26/archives/jack-kapp-headed-decca-relords-47-founder- of-company-in-1933-dies.html.

49 Cary Ginell, *Milton Brown and the Founding of Western Swing* (University of Illinois, 1994), 167.

50 N. Hudson, "Story of Sound, Part 3: Shellac to Vinyl—How World War Two changed the Record," *Norfolk Record Office*, October 10, 2020, norfolkrecordofficeblog.org/2020/10/10/story-of-sound-part-3-shellac-to-vinyl-how- world-war-two-changed-the-record.

51 "The President's National Medal of Science: Recipient Details—Peter C. Goldmark," National Science Foundation, www.nsf.gov/od/nms/recip_details.jsp?recip_id=140.

52 "Invention," *History of the LP Record*, lprecord.umwblogs.org/history/invention.

53 Scott Thill, "June 21, 1948: Columbia's Microgroove LP Makes Albums Sound Good," *Wired*, June 21, 2010, www.wired.com/2010/06/0621first-lp-released.

54 Ibid.

55 Gideon Schwartz, *Hi-Fi: The History of High-End Audio Design* (Phaidon, 2019), 10–11, 27.

56 Music in the Mail, "The following narrative was told by Edward Wallerstein (1891–1970) about the development of the LP record in 1948," *Music in the Mail*, www.musicinthemail.com/audiohistoryLP.html.

57 Michael Greig Thomas, "The Resurgence of the Vinyl Single: The 7" 45rpm Record," June 28, 2016, www.linkedin.com/pulse/resurgence-vinyl-single-7-45rpm-record-michael-greig-thomas.

58 Sean Wilentz, "The Birth of 33⅓," *Slate*, November 2, 2012, www.slate.com/articles/arts/books/2012/11/birth_of_the_long_playing_record_plus_rare_photos_from_the_heyday_of_columbia.html.

59 Guy A. Marco, ed., *Encyclopedia of Recorded Sound in the United States* (New York and London: Garland, 1993), worldradiohistory.com/BOOKSHELF-ARH/Encyclopedias/Miscellaneous-Encyclopedias/Encyclopedia-of-Recorded-Sound-in-the%20United-States-Marco-19.pdf.

60 Music in the Mail.

61 Ibid.

62 David Browne, "How the 45 RPM Single Changed Music Forever," *Rolling Stone*, March 15, 2019, www.rollingstone.com/music/music-features/45-vinyl-singles-history-806441.

63 "The First New York Audio Fair: the Annual Convention of the Audio Engineering Society, Oct. 27–29, 1949," *Leak and the Audio Engineering Society New York Audio Fairs*, www.44bx.com/leak/exhibitions.html.

64 Jeffrey K. Ziesmann, "Milton B Sleeper," *World Radio History*, worldradiohistory.com/Archive-FM-Magazine/MiltonSleeperBio.htm.

65 Greg Milner, *Perfecting Sound Forever: An Aural History of Recorded Music* (Farrar, Straus and Giroux, 2009), 35.

66 "Collaro Ltd.," *Gramophone Museum*, www.gramophonemuseum.com/collaro.html.

67 "Philco NOS vintage record player, model M-15," RadiolaGuy.com, www.radiolaguy.com/Showcase/Audio/Philco_M-15.htm.

68 "Why When 45 RPM Vinyl Singles and Their Record Players Debuted, It Was a Big Deal," *Click Americana*, clickamericana.com/media/music/new-rca-victor-45-automatic-record-changer-1949.

69 Brian Coleman, "The Technics 1200—Hammer Of The Gods," *Medium*, January 6, 2016, medium.com/@briancoleman/the-technics-1200-hammer-of-the-gods-xxl-fall-1998-5b93180a67da.

70 Pat Blashill, "Six Machines That Changed The Music World," *Wired*, May 1, 2002, www.wired.com/2002/05/blackbox.

71 Hans Fantel, *ABC's of HiFi Stereo*, 2nd ed. (Howard W. Sams, 1967), 12.

72 Hans Fantel, "100 Years Ago: The Beginning of Stereo," *New York Times*, January 4, 1981, www.nytimes.com/1981/01/04/arts/100-years-ago-the-beginning-of-stereo.html.

73 "Alan Blumlein and the Invention of Stereo," *EMI Archive Trust*, December 16, 2013, www.emiarchivetrust.org/alan-blumlein-and-the-invention-of-stereo.

74 William E. Garity and J. N. A. Hawkins, "Fantasound," *Journal of the Society of Motion Picture Engineers* 37, no. 8 (August 1941), doi:10.5594/J12890.

75 "Updated: Emory Cook, Binaural Recording Pioneer," *Preservation Sound*, November 16, 2012, www.preservationsound.com/2012/11/emory-cook-binaural-recording-pioneer. "Cook's Choice," *Sound Fountain*, www.soundfountain.com/cook/cook-livingston-binaural.html.

76 "Arnold Sugden: Pioneer of Single-Groove Stereo," *Electronics World and Wireless World*, June 1994, worldradiohistory.com/hd2/IDX-UK/Technology/Technology-All-Eras/Archive-Wireless-World-IDX/90s/Wireless-World-1994-06-OCR-Page-0048.pdf.

77 Susan Schmidt Horning, *Chasing Sound: Technology, Culture and the Art of Studio Recording from Edison to the LP* (Baltimore: Johns Hopkins University, 2013), x, 292.

78 "Jack Mullin," *History of Recording*, www.historyofrecording.com/Jack_Mullin.html.

79 John Leslie and Ross Snyder, "History of The Early Days of Ampex Corporation," *AES Historical Committee*, December 17, 2010, www.aes.org/aeshc/docs/company.histories/ampex/leslie_snyder_early-days-of-ampex.pdf. "In Memoriam: Ross H. Snyder 1920–2008," *Journal of the Audio Engineering Society* 56, nos. 1/2 (January/February 2008), www.aes.org/aeshc/jaes.obit/JAES_V56_1_2_PG100.pdf.

80 Steven E. Schoenherr, "Stereophonic Sound," *AES Media*, www.aes-media.org/historical/html/recording.technology.history/stereo.html.

81 Jared Hobbs, "RIAA Curve: The 1954 Turntable Equalization Standard That Still Matters," *LedgerNote*, August 27, 2021, www.ledgernote.com/columns/mixing-mastering/riaa-curve/ledgernote.com/columns/mixing-mastering/riaa-curve.

82 "Is it a Linn or An Ariston?," *Linn Sondek*, July 12, 2011, linnsondek.wordpress.com.

83 "Transcriptors Hydraulic Reference Turntable as Seen in *A Clockwork Orange*," *Film and Furniture*, filmandfurniture.com/product/transcriptors-hydraulic-reference-turntable-as-seen-in-a-clockwork-orange.

84 "The Thorens TD 124 Page," *Sound Fountain*, www.soundfountain.com/amb/td124page.html.

85 "Recording: While My Guitar Gently Weeps," *The Beatles Bible*, August 15, 2018, www.beatlesbible.com/1968/08/16/recording-while-my-guitar-gently-weeps-2.

86 Greg Milner, *Perfecting Sound Forever* (New York: Farrar, Straus, and Giroux, 2009), 160.

87 "Akai Electric Company Ltd.," *Museum of Magnetic Sound Recording*, museumofmagneticsoundrecording.org/ManufacturersAkai.html.

88 "Jacob Jensen, Beogram 4000 Record Player, 1972," *Museum of Modern Art*, www.moma.org/collection/works/2483; "Jacob Jensen, Beogram 6000 Turntable, 1974," *Museum of Modern Art*, www.moma.org/collection/works/2161.

89 Steve Guttenberg, "100 Years of Denon," *CNET*, August 23, 2010, www.cnet.com/tech/home-entertainment/100-years-of-denon.

90 "110th Anniversary Of Denon Vol.2 Interview With Ryo Okazeri, The Record Player Engineer," *Denon*, www.denon.com/de-ch/blog/110th-anniversary-of-denon-vol-2-interview-with-ryo-okazeri-the-record-player-engineer.

91 Ibid.

92 "Hi-Fi that Rocked the World," *Hi-fi Choice*, July 20, 2006, archived at the Wayback Machine, web.archive.org/web/20070718222232/http://www.hifichoice.co.uk/page/hifichoice?entry=hi_fi_that_rocked_the.

93 "The Ten Most Significant Turntables of All Time," *The Absolute Sound*, no. 216 (September 11, 2017), archived at the Wayback Machine, web.archive.org/web/20140201223153/http://www.avguide.com/review/the-ten-most-significant-turntables-all-time-tas-216?page=1.

94 Optonica sales catalogue, OP-FB 10/77, 26–27.

95 "Brian Eno - in conference with CompuServe on July 4th, 1996 at his London studio," *Hyperreal Music Archive*, music.hyperreal.org/artists/brian_eno/interviews/ciseno.html.

96 Trevor Pinch and, Karin Bijsterveld, *The Oxford Handbook of Sound Studies* (Oxford University Press, 2011), 515; Todd Souvingier, *The World of DJs and the Turntable Culture*, (Hal Leonard Corporation, 2003), 43.

97 Max Mahood, "Wheels of Steel: The Story of the Technics SL-1200," *Happy*, October 7, 2018, happymag.tv/technics-sl-1200.

98 "The Complete Technics SL1200 Turntable Guide," *We Are Crossfader*, July 28, 2020, wearecrossfader.co.uk/blog/the-complete-technics-sl1200-turntable-guide.

99 "The Source: History," *The Source Turntable*, December 28, 2011, thesourceturntable.blogspot.com/search/label/Source%20History%20Overview.

100 John Atkinson, "Pierre Lurne: Audiomeca's Turntable Designer," *Stereophile*, September 7, 2010 (first published December 7, 1987), www.stereophile.com/interviews/pierre_lurne_audiomecas_turntable_designer/index.html.

101 "Reference: Collectors' Items of Extreme Rarity and Value," *Goldmund*, goldmund.com/reference-turntable-dvdplayer.

102 All-Akustik, "The Philosophy of Perfection," product catalog, 2–3, www.vinylengine.com/ve_downloads/index.php?micro_seiki/micro_seiki_philosophie_catalog_de.pdf.

103 Ibid.

104 Steve Harris, "Oracle Delphi," *Hi-Fi News*, April 2013, docs.wixstatic.com/ugd/a191a2_addf52ce14434afdaf89ae8b29a949b9.pdf.

105 Malcolm Steward "Pink Triangle," *High Fidelity*, June 1990, www.topaudiogear.com/index.php/interviews-hi-fis-celebrities/pink-triangle-1990.

106 Craig Kalman, email to author, January 9, 2022.

107 "Introduction," *Eminent Technology*, www.eminent-tech.com/history/eminenthistory.htm.

108 "Jacob Jensen," *Bang & Olufsen*, www.bang-olufsen.com/en/us/story/jacob-jensen-design-icon.

109 Karl Henkell, *Record*, no. 6 (2019), 10.

110 "4724 Koma Turntable," *Sakura Systems Presents 47 Laboratory*, www.sakurasystems.com/reference/koma.html.

111 "Mark Döhmann Bio," *Döhmann*, dohmannaudio.com/mark-dohmann.

112 "Clearaudio Statement TT-1 Tangential Tonearm," *Musical Surroundings*, www.musicalsurroundings.com/products/clearaudio-statement-tt1-tangential-tonearm.

113 "Gabriel / DaVinciAudio Reference Turntable MKII," *DaVinciAudio Labs*, da-vinci-audio.com/davinciaudio20aas20gabriel20mk220turntablehtml.

114 "Circle 25 Turntable & A.C.T. 25 Tonearm," *Wilson Benesch White Papers*, wilson-benesch.com/wp-content/themes/mxp_base_theme/mxp_theme/assets/wilson_benesch_circle25_white_paper_lr.pdf.

115 "Rega P3-24 review," *TechRadar*, February 8, 2007, http://www.techradar.com/reviews/audio-visual/hi-fi-and-audio/turntables/rega-p3-24-102104/review, archived from the original on November 21, 2013.

116 "Aeroarm," *Simon Yorke Designs*, www.recordplayer.com/webant/en/turntable/aeroarm/specifications.html.

117 "Walker Audio Proscenium Black Diamond V," *Robb Report*, robbreport.com/gear/electronics/slideshow/10-most-over-top-turntables-world/walker-audio-proscenium-black-diamond-v.

118 "The Walker Proscenium Black Diamond VI Master Reference," *Walker Audio*, walkeraudio.com/proscenium-black-diamond-v.

119 "Awards," *Walker Audio*, walkeraudio.com/awards.

120 Art Dudley, "Roksan Kandy K2 Integrated Amplifier," *Stereophile*, May 15, 2010, www.stereophile.com/integratedamps/roksan_kandy_k2_integrated_amplifier/index.html.

121 Ketan Bharadia, "Touraj Moghaddam: The Man Behind Roksan and Vertere Talks Turntables and Cables," *What Hi-Fi?*, March 4, 2020, www.whathifi.com/us/features/touraj-moghaddam-the-man-behind-roksan-and-vertere-talks-turntables-and-cables.

○○   Author's Acknowledgments

First and foremost I would like to thank my wife, Alissa, and three children, Zoey, Violet, and Henry. While certainly worthwhile, this was a daunting and time-consuming endeavor, regrettably taking my attention away from you— but never without your patience, support, and encouragement. It must be challenging to have a lunatic record collector audiophile as a husband and father, so I am indebted to you for your compassion. To my beautiful parents, whom I cherish and love dearly; but they still haven't come to terms with me quitting law to sell stereos and scribble. Heartfelt thanks to Alan and Nancy for their ceaseless love, inspiration, and faith in me. To my singularly discerning and dear friend Michael Maharam, whose Lower East Side roots will always be his best part. Virginia McLeod, my fearless commissioning editor at Phaidon, had the foresight and depth to envision audio as a distinct art form, meriting my second book on the subject. Absolutely indispensable was Phaidon senior editor Maia Murphy, whose acumen, keen eye for design, and, most importantly, cracking the whip to meet deadlines has left me eternally in awe (fear) of her. Lastly are my friends Ron Meador and Nelson Brill, living, breathing music encyclopedias from whom I have learned so much, fostering my own musical exploration, awareness, and growth.

○○   Publisher's Acknowledgments

The publisher would like to extend special thanks to Sarah Bell, Vanessa Bird, Clive Burroughs, Garlia Cornelia, Vishwa Kaushal, Deanna Lee, Laine Morreau, Mat Smith, and Sarah Tucker for their contributions to the book, as well as Mark Lott, Stuart Knapman, and Mark Robson at Altaimage for their incredible pre-press work.

○○   About the Author

Born and based in New York, Gideon Schwartz is a former attorney who retired from practicing law in 2009 to pursue his passion for the highest-fidelity audio equipment. To this end, Schwartz founded his company, Audioarts, in 2010, through which he sells ultra-high-end audio designs to those seeking the utmost fidelity. With an emphasis on conveying what he calls "musical truth," Schwartz champions equipment that can provide users with ethereal audio experiences alongside equal deference to high-quality industrial design and construction. In merging the presentation of the musical arts with high-end domestic sound reproduction, Audioarts strives to preserve the artist's spirit and intent. Schwartz is the author of the book *Hi-Fi: The History of High-End Audio Design*, published by Phaidon in 2019.

Phaidon Press Limited
2 Cooperage Yard
London E15 2QR

Phaidon Press Inc.
111 Broadway
New York, NY 10006

phaidon.com

First published 2022
Reprinted 2024
© 2022 Phaidon Press Limited

ISBN 978 1 83866 561 6

Commissioning Editor: Virginia McLeod
Project Editor: Maia Murphy
Production Controller: Sarah Kramer and Marina Asenjo
Design: Amaury Hamon for (Studio) Jonathan Hares

Printed in China